CALIFORNIA WATER
A New Political Economy

Today while great concern is felt for the diminishing supply of the earth's resources, little attention is given the role of political systems in the distribution of those resources. This study examines governmental control of the allocation of a basic resource—water—in the state of California. Over 1,000 water districts are examined, employing over 100 financial variables and covering a period of ten years. Patterns of financial and political performance in each of the districts are compared and the impact of different political decision systems upon district functioning is measured. The study is concerned with the productivity of contrasting types of water districts. But it is also sensitive to questions of equity and of distribution: What economic and political mechanisms facilitate the flow and control of benefits and costs? Who benefits from the development of water resources? Who pays the cost of development? This is a study in political economy and water districts in California are described in terms of both political characteristics and major financial indicators.

CALIFORNIA WATER

A New Political Economy

by
MERRILL R. GOODALL
JOHN D. SULLIVAN
TIMOTHY DE YOUNG

LandMark Studies
ALLANHELD, OSMUN / UNIVERSE BOOKS
Montclair and New York

ALLANHELD, OSMUN AND CO. PUBLISHERS, INC.
19 Brunswick Road, Montclair, N.J. 07042
Published in the United States of America in 1978
by Allanheld, Osmun and Co. and by Universe Books
381 Park Avenue South, New York, N.Y. 10016
Distribution: Universe Books

Copyright © 1978 Merrill R. Goodall, John D. Sullivan, Timothy De Young

All rights reserved. No part of this publication may be reproduced, stored in a
retrieval system, or transmitted in any form or by any means, electronic, mechanical,
photocopying, recording, or otherwise, without prior permission of the publisher.

Goodall, Merrill R
   California water.

   (LandMark studies)
   Includes index.
   1. Water resources development—California.
I. Sullivan, John D., joint author. II. De Young,
Timothy, joint author. III. Title.
HD1694.C2G66   333.9'1'009794   77-88255
ISBN 0-87663-827-2

Printed in the United States of America

Preface and Acknowledgements

Today, while great concern is felt for the diminishing supply of the earth's resources, little attention is given to the role of political systems in the distribution of those resources. This study examines the way in which California governmental institutions control the allocation of a basic resource, water. Over 1,000 water districts are examined, employing over 100 financial variables and covering a period of 10 years. Patterns of financial and political performance in each of the districts are compared and the impact of different political decision systems upon district functioning is measured. We are concerned with the productivity of contrasting types of water districts. But we are also sensitive to questions of equity and of distribution and we ask: What economic and political mechanisms facilitate the flow and control of benefits and costs? Who benefits from the development of water resources? Who pays the cost of development? This is a study in political economy and we describe water districts in California in terms of both political characteristics and major financial indicators.

We would like to thank the staff of the Seaver Computer Center for the technical assistance which they provided. Most of the data presented in this study was analyzed on the Seaver Computer Center PDP DEC10 system using the Statistical Package for the Social Sciences.

Ours has been a genuinely collaborative study. We are glad to acknowledge the assistance of the Department of Water Resources of the State of California. We have been aided by many and it is impossible to name all who contributed to our work. We especially wish to thank Aubrey Birkelbach, Phil Cohen, Betsy Goodall, Jim Jamieson, Dave Martin, Del Read, Pete Steinbroner, Alicia Thompson, Stella Vlastos and Bruce Wilson. The graphics in Chapter 3 were done by Ben Bull. The authors alone are responsible for the present text.

Contents

List of Tables and Figures	viii
1. The Institutional Setting	3
2. Patterns of Financial Performance: General Description and Trends	29
3. Patterns of Financial Performance: Correlation Analysis and Proportions	53
4. A New Political Economy	95
Appendices	
A. Classification of Counties by Percent Urban	101
B. Methodological Note	102
C. List of Variables	107
D. Variables and Formulae Used in Chapter 3	110
E. Abbreviations of Districts Used in Tables	113
Index	115
About the Authors	118

LIST OF TABLES AND FIGURES

Table

1-1	Water Districts by Type of Enabling Legislation and Number of Districts, 1970-71 and 1974-75	6
1-2	Incorporation of Water Districts by Decade, 1880-1970, and by Type of Act	8
1-3	Principal Acts Employed in Creating Districts 1880-1949 and 1950-69	10
1-4	Trends in Type of Service Provided by Water Districts in California, 1880-1970	11
1-5	Property Qualification Required in Incorporation Procedure of Districts 1880-1949 and 1950-70	12
1-6	Property Qualification for Electors in Districts 1880-1949 and 1950-70	13
1-7	Incorporation of Districts by Geographic Setting, 1880-1970	14
1-8	Activities not Directly Related to Water Use Engaged in by Districts Conducting Water Utility Operations, 1970-71	17
1-9	Elections of Water District Directors, by Type of District, 1973 and 1975	19
1-10	Elections in Water Storage Districts, 1973 and 1975: Number of Uncontested and Contested Elections and Number of Available Seats and Candidates	22
1-11	Elections in Water Storage Districts, 1969 and 1971: Number of Uncontested and Contested Elections and Number of Available Seats and Candidates	23
1-12	Elections in Water Storage Districts, 1965 and 1967: Number of Uncontested and Contested Elections and Number of Available Seats and Candidates	24
1-13	Berrenda Mesa Water District; Landowners with Holdings Exceeding 500 Acres, 1976	26
1-14	Berrenda Mesa Water District: Type of Landowner, 1973-1976	27
2-1	Frequency of Financial Reporting to the State Controller: Irrigation Districts and California Water Districts	30
2-2	Average Acreage by Type of District	34
2-3	Average District Revenues by Type of District	36

List of tables and Figures ix

2-4	Average Revenues from Levies by Type of District	38
2-5	Average Rates of Levy by Type of District	40
2-6	Average Debt, Total Outstanding, Longterm by Type of District	42
2-7	Average Total Expenditures by Type of District	44
2-8	Average Expenditure-Capital Outlay by Type of District	49
2-9 thru 2-13	Acreage Total Revenue and Revenue from Levy Assessment Averages by Method of Selection of Governing Body	50
3-1	The Correlation of Indebtedness, Revenue and Expenditure with Acreage by Method of Selection of Governing Body	56
3-2	The Correlation of Indebtedness, Revenue and Expenditure by Method of Selection of Governing Body	58
3-3	The Correlation of Revenue with Expenditure by Method of Selection of Governing Body and by Type of County	60
3-4	The Correlation of Indebtedness with Acreage by Method of Selection of Governing Body and by Type of County	61
3-5	The Correlation of Revenue with Acreage by Method of Selection of Governing Body and by type of County	62
3-6	The Correlation of Expenditure with Acreage Method of Selection of Governing Body and by Type of County	64
3-7	The Correlation of Revenue with Indebtedness Method of Selection of Governing Body and by Type of County	65
3-8	The Correlation of Expenditure with Indebtedness, Method of Selection of Governing Body and by Type of County	66
3-9	Net Operating Income-or Loss-As a Proportion of Total Revenues by Type of District and by Method of Selection of Governing Body	69
3-10	Sales Revenue Proportion of Total Revenues by Method of Selection and by Type of County	70
3-11	Sales Revenue Proportion of Total Revenues by Type of District	71
3-12	Domestic and Irrigation Sales Revenue Proportion of Total Sales Revenues for 1968 and 1970 by Type of District	72
3-13	Levy Revenue Proportion of Total Revenues by Method of Selection of Governing Body and by Type of County	74
3-14	Levy Revenue Proportion of Total Revenues by Type of District	75
3-15	a. Depreciation, Amortization Expenditure Proportion of Total Operating Expenditures by Type of District	76
	b. Utility Depletion Additions Expenditure Proportion of Total Expenditure by Type of District	76
3-16	Net Operating Income-or Loss-As a Proportion of Total Revenues by Type of District and by Method of Selection of Governing Body	78

x *List of Tables and Figures*

3-17	Levy Revenue Proportion of Total Revenues by Method of Selection of Governing Body and by Type of County	79
3-18	Levy Revenue Proportion of Total Revenues by Type of District	80
3-19	Sales Revenue Proportion of Total Revenues by Type of District	81
3-20	Districts With Significant Differences by Count (P≤.05)	82
3-21	Administrative Expenditure Proportion of Total Expenditures by Method of Selection of Governing Body and by Type of County	84
3-22	Administrative Expenditure Proportion of Total Expenditures by Type of District	85
3-23	The Relative and Absolute Frequency of Differing Levy Revenue Proportion Levels in 1970 by Type of District and by Method of Selection of Governing Body	89

Figure

1	Revenue Plotted Against Acreage Irrigation Districts	90
2	Revenue Plotted Against Acreage-California Water Districts	91
3	Expenditures Plotted Against Acreage Irrigation Districts	92
4	Expenditures Plotted Against Acreage-California Water Districts	93

CALIFORNIA WATER

CHAPTER

1

The Institutional Setting

California's history has been characterized by bitter competition for scarce water resources. In recent decades that competition has intensified as a result of very substantial new agricultural development on the west side of the San Joaquin Valley. Domestic and industrial requirements, particularly in semi-arid southern California, continue to increase. The 1975–77 drought, the most severe in the state's history, led to emergency regulations, further exacerbated traditional regional rivalries, and stimulated newer patterns of competition between agrarian and urban use and between large-scale agriculture and family-size farming.

Water distribution has profoundly influenced urban development in California and has fostered the growth of two distinctive, co-existing political systems in rural California. One political system, most evident on the eastern side of the San Joaquin Valley and throughout much of the Sacramento Valley, is characterized by one person/one vote political institutions and large-scale corporate agriculture.

The eastern sides of the San Joaquin and Sacramento Valleys were settled in the late nineteenth century and irrigation agriculture in these areas was dependent first on ground water reserves and the flow of streams with origins in the adjacent Sierra. Water impoundment and water delivery systems were next constructed, administered, and paid for by a new type of public agency, the Irrigation District. Irrigation Districts were authorized by the Wright Act of 1887, the state legislature's first comprehensive enabling act for water district organization. Voting for directors of Irrigation Districts is based on one vote for each registered eligible voter. Today farm size in areas governed by Irrigation Districts tends to be relatively small and farming is typically in the hands of residents. Voter turnout in elections for district directors is comparatively high.

Agricultural development in the western and southern areas of the San Joaquin was accomplished in relatively recent times. Indeed, the west side was brought under cultivation only in the past 15 to 20 years. Agriculture is in the hands generally of large-scale, non-resident entities. Corporate holdings in excess of 10,000 acres are not uncommon and may measure as much as 100,000 acres. One public institution which facilitates this type of resource development is the California Water District, a special district first authorized by the state legislature in 1913. In such districts, voting is weighted by property; each voter may cast one vote for each dollar's worth of land to which he holds title and owners of land, both resident and non-resident in the district, may vote on questions of district formation and the incurring of bonded indebtedness. Contested elections in such districts are rare and turnout is low. The system of irrigation in many of the property qualification districts is frequently dependent on federally funded hydraulic systems, the most notable being the United States Bureau of Reclamation's San Luis Project, which serves the 600,000-acre Westlands District.

WATER DISTRICT ENABLING ACTS AND THEIR EVOLUTION[1]

California's growing population and the increase in agricultural and industrial activity in the state have been matched by an increase in the number of institutions designed to supply water to different types of consumers. Water districts in California are in effect governments with a wide array of powers. In this section we classify water districts by type of enabling act, by type of governing body, by indicators of citizen involvement, and by geographic locale. We measure change in reliance on contrasting enabling acts, in systems of election, in type of agricultural settlement, in use of land and water, and in effect of scale of agricultural operation on community organization. Our focus is the institutional setting of water development.

More than 1,000 public and private agencies share responsibility for the administration of California's water resources. Those agencies are both federal and state and include municipal water departments operated by such governments of general jurisdiction as cities and counties. Among the agencies are privately owned enterprises under public regulation and mutual water companies. Also included are those special districts which conduct water utility operations. Special districts enjoy a unique role in the administration of water resources in California. Today more than 900 special districts in California perform water utility functions. These districts are legally constituted governmental entities, created under either general or special acts of the state legislature and governed by a body established by the statute which formed the district. The governing body may be independent and elected by its constituency, or it may be dependent, in which case the county board of supervisors, or in some cases the city council, manages its affairs. Such districts are ordinarily authorized to levy taxes, issue both general obligation and revenue bonds, and set rates for services. In recent decades these districts, although charged most prominently with water resource activities, tend to assume many of the features of general municipal governments and provide the basic services normally engaged in by cities.

Our analysis encompasses only those special districts which conduct water functions. In 1970–71 there were 4,235 special districts in California, not including school districts; the 886 water districts operating at that time constituted about 21 percent of all special districts. In 1974–75 the total number reached 4,650 and 908, or 19.5 percent, were water districts. There has been a steady increase in the number of special districts since 1945, with the proportion of water districts to the total number remaining fairly stable.

General enabling acts of the state legislature provide for 17 classes of special districts with water utility functions. Other districts with

Table 1-1

WATER DISTRICTS BY TYPE OF ENABLING LEGISLATION AND
NUMBER OF DISTRICTS, 1970-71 and 1974-75

Type of District	General Law or Code	Code Section	No. of Districts 1970-71	No. of Districts 1974-75
1. Community Services[a]	Government	61000 et seq	103	116
2. Flood Control & Water Conservation	General laws	b	7	8
3. Harbors & Ports	Harbors & navig.	6200 et seq	1	1
4. Municipal Improvement	General laws	b	4	4
5. Maintenance	Sts. & hwys.	5820 et seq	33	34
6. Reclamation	Water	50000 et seq	8	10
7. Recreation & Parks[c]	Public resources	5780 et seq	6	6
8. County Service Area	Government	25210.1 et seq	28	43
9. Municipal Utility	Public utilities	11501 et seq	3	3
10. Public Utility[d]	Public utilities	15501 et seq	52	52
11. California Water	Water	34000 et seq	160	162
12. County Water	Water	30000 et seq	192	189
13. Metropolitan	General laws	e	1	1
14. Municipal Water	Water	71000 et seq	50	47
15. Water Agency or Authority	General laws	b	24	27
16. Water Conservation	Water	74000 et seq	8	11
17. Water Replenishment	Water	60000 et seq	1	1
18. Water Storage	Water	39000 et seq	8	8
19. County Waterworks	Water	55000 et seq	90	88
20. Irrigation	Water	20500 et seq	107	103

a. includes one special-act district
b. special-act districts only
c. includes four special-act districts
d. includes two special-act districts
e. includes Metropolitan Water District only

water resource responsibilities have been established by special act of the legislature; these special-act districts, which may be classified by three functional categories, are included in our analysis. We exclude from our analysis all municipal water departments, privately owned agencies, and certain general-act and special-act districts that perform only inconsequential water services. The 20 types of districts are briefly identified in Table 1-1. That table also notes the number of districts of each type for the years 1970-71 and 1974-75. The short descriptive label given each type of district in Table 1-1 is drawn from the legislative enactment and should be seen only as a general indicator of the type of water services. Certain special-act districts are numbered within a few of the general enabling act classes; a few special-act districts are included in the count for Community Service Districts, Recreation and Parks Districts, and Public Utility Districts. All of the districts described as Flood Control and Water Conservation, Municipal Improvement, and Water Agency or Authority are special-act districts. Only one district is classed within the Metropolitan Water District Act.

Special districts with water resource responsibilities reflect the varying needs of agricultural, commercial, and industrial enterprises and have been shaped most significantly in this century by demands from a developing corporate agriculture and the state's densely populated water-deficit areas. Such districts range in size from a small Irrigation District to the Metropolitan Water District of California, which "has had the strength to affect the development of practically all of the area south of the Tehachapis, containing approximately one half of the people of California and one half of the state's tax resources."[2]

The first comprehensive enabling act for water district organization mirrored agrarian purposes; the 1887 Wright Act authorized Irrigation Districts and irrigation was the dominant purpose of districts created up until the middle of the twentieth century. The Wright Act was used but sparingly in the two decades following 1950. A general perspective on the developmental purpose of water districts is afforded by Table 1-2, which accounts for the incorporation of districts by type of act and by decade for the period 1880-1970. Table 1-2 accommodates districts created by special legislative act as well as those formed under the general enabling acts. The shifting reliance on types of enabling statutes, shown in Table 1-2, is closely related to basic changes in the state's economy,

Table 1-2

INCORPORATION OF WATER DISTRICTS BY DECADE,
1880-1970, AND BY TYPE OF ACT

Decade	1	2	3	4	5	6	7	8	9	10	11	12	13	14	15	16	17	18	19	20	Decade Totals
1880-89																				5	5
1890-99																				1	1
1900-09																				2	2
1910-19				1								3		1					2	23	30
1920-29				3			1	7		1	9	1				2		2	5	44	75
1930-39	1						1	10		2	8					1		1	4	4	32
1940-49		1						25		9	18		2		1			1	4	8	69
1950-59	38	2	2	2			1	7		69	77		29	11	3	1		3	30	8	283
1960-69	56	1		2	8		5	19		2	72	72	17	9				1	21	1	285
1970	14			1			8				4	8		2	1	1			2	1	42
	109	3	1	4	11	4	5	27	3	51	156	195	1	51	21	8	1	8	68	97	824
No date No file	1	5			25	5	1	6		1	5					4	2		24	10	89
Dissolved	2										11		3		2			2	2		22

a. Type of enabling act:

1. Community Services
2. Flood Control and Water Conservation
3. Harbors and Ports
4. Municipal Improvement
5. Maintenance
6. Reclamation
7. Recreation and Park
8. County Service Areas
9. Municipal Utility
10. Public Utility
11. California Water
12. County Water
13. Metropolitan Water
14. Municipal Water
15. Water Agency or Authority
16. Water Conservation
17. Water Replenishment
18. Water Storage
19. County Waterworks
20. Irrigation

b. Numbers do not coincide with tabulations in Controller's Annual Reports, which are based on districts submitting data on financial transactions.

Source: Files at the offices of the State Controller and the Secretary of State, Sacramento.

to the growth of population in the state, and to concentration of population in urban areas. The two decades from 1950–70 were exceptionally active; 283 districts were incorporated in the 1950s and 285 were incorporated in the 1960s. Five of the enabling acts provided the statutory base for the creation of as many as 196 districts in the 1950s and 206 districts in the 1960s. These five enabling acts are designated in Table 1-2 as Community Services, California Water, County Service Area, Municipal Water, and County Waterworks Districts. These districts share several significant characteristics. They are competent to deal with all uses of water. Three types (Community Services, County Service Area, and County Water District) are employed primarily in unincorporated areas to provide basic services normally provided by cities. Two of the five of these enabling acts used most frequently in recent years (Community Services and California Water) require landowner participation in the formation process and one (California Water) requires land ownership as a qualification for voting for the governing directors of the district. In all of the five districts popular in the period 1950–70, the governing body is accorded considerable rule-making authority.

It is apparent from our tabular summaries that most water districts are of recent vintage and that a steadily decreasing share relates primarily to the agricultural function. Although as much as 85 percent of the water used in the state today is for irrigation purposes (and public districts account for more than three quarters of the agricultural acreage), a decline in the relative importance of such use as a consequence of increasing urbanization can be anticipated. And, not surprisingly, Irrigation Districts are increasingly delivering water for domestic and industrial purposes. A comparison of the principal acts employed in authorizing districts in the periods 1880–1949 and 1950–69 underscores the movement of these water institutions from a rural setting to one that is urbanizing and industrial (see Table 1-3). As shown in this table, prior to 1950, 214 districts on which incorporation dates are availalbe were formed under a major enabling act. However, in two decades alone, from 1950–70, 610 districts were formed. Of the 214 districts established up to 1950, 167, or 78 percent, were drawn from three enabling acts; Irrigation Districts accounted for 87, Puclic Utility Districts for 42, and County Water Districts for 38. Both the Irrigation and the Public Utility Districts undertook functions related mainly to

Table 1-3

PRINCIPAL ACTS EMPLOYED IN CREATING DISTRICTS
1880-1949 and 1950-69

YEARS		ENABLING ACT	TIMES EMPLOYED	PERCENT-AGE
1880-1949	214 districts created, including	Irrigation	87	40.7
		Public Utility	42	19.6
		County Water	38	17.8
1950-69	610 districts created, including	County Water	157	25.7
		California Water	145	24.7
		Community Services	108	17.7

Source: Compiled from files at the offices of the State Controller and the Secretary of State, Sacramento.

agriculture. Of the 610 districts formed between 1950 and 1970, three acts led to 410 districts, or 68 percent of the total; there were 157 new County Water Districts, 145 California Water Districts, and 108 Community Services Districts. For some California Water Districts that began operating in the 1950–70 period, water for irrigation was the rationale. Irrigation use has been a factor in several of the latter-day County Water Districts but could not have led to formation of the Community Services Districts. When the functions of districts formed from the 1880s to 1970 are classified as (1) primarily irrigation use, (2) irrigation and urban use, and (3) urban use only, the declining number of types of districts serving agriculture is apparent (see Table 1-4).

Although many of the districts formed in recent decades assume many of the features of general governments, there is also a tendency to form districts under those enabling acts which require landowner participation in the formation of the district and property qualification for participation in elections to the governing body of the district. Six enabling acts require property ownership for incorporators of districts. These classes of districts are Community Services, Water Storage, Irrigation, Reclamation,

Table 1-4

TRENDS IN TYPE OF SERVICE PROVIDED BY WATER DISTRICTS
IN CALIFORNIA, 1880-1970

Decade	Primarily Irrigation		Irrigation and Urban		Urban Only	
	Number	Percent for Decade	Number	Percent for Decade	Number	Percent for Decade
1880-89	5	100.0	0	0.0	0	0.0
1890-99	1	100.0	0	0.0	0	0.0
1900-09	2	100.0	0	0.0	0	0.0
1910-19	24	80.0	6	20.0	0	0.0
1920-29	56	74.6	11	14.6	8	10.8
1930-39	5	15.6	16	50.1	11	34.4
1940-49	8	11.6	33	47.9	28	40.5
1950-59	8	2.8	196	69.0	79	28.2
1960-69	1	0.2	175	61.4	109	38.4
1970-	1	2.4	12	28.5	29	69.1

Sources: Files at the offices of the State Controller and the Secretary of State, Sacramento; classification of districts drawn from language of enabling legislation and financial transactions of the districts.

California Water, and Water Conservation. Four general enabling acts established property ownership as a requirement for voting. These are the acts authorizing California Water Districts, Reclamation Districts, Water Storage Districts, and certain Water Conservation Districts. Several special act districts also set property ownership as a prerequisite to voting. In property qualification districts, property owners vote on the basis of the amount of property they own or its value. In all Reclamation Districts and California Water Districts landowners receive one vote for each one dollar of the assessed value of their land. Landowners in Water Storage Districts are granted one vote for each $100 of their land's assessed value (exclusive of improvements, minerals, and mineral rights). And some Water Conservation Districts are property-

Table 1-5

PROPERTY QUALIFICATION REQUIRED IN INCORPORATION

PROCEDURE OF DISTRICTS

1880-1949 and 1950-70

Years	Number of Districts[a]	Districts with Property Requirements in Incorporation Procedure[b]	Percentage
1880-1949	214	72	33.1
1950-69	610	310	50.8

a. Includes districts with known dates of incorporation.

b. Source of classification: enabling legislation. Property qualification for petitioners is required in the following classes of districts: Community Services, Water Storage, Irrigation, Reclamation, California Water, Water Conservation.

weighted districts; for example, the 1927 enabling act for Water Conservation Districts gives each landowner one vote for each acre of land owned, or one vote if the land owned is less than one acre. About one fifth of all water districts in the state now require property qualification for voting. As shown in Table 1-5, 72 or 33.1 percent of the districts formed between 1880 and 1949 required a property qualification of petitioners for incorporation; from 1950-69, 310 or 50.8 percent of the districts demanded propertied petitioners. We note a more marked increase when we follow the formation of districts that require property qualification for voting; in the 1950-69 period, 155 or 25.4 percent of the districts formed required property qualification (see Table 1-6).

When the incorporation dates of districts are classified by geographic setting, yet another trend is apparent. The earliest districts, which were generally Irrigation Districts, were located in the Sacramento Valley and the northern and eastern reaches of the San Joaquin Valley. Since 1950, however, the vast majority of new districts have been incorporated in southern California and in the San Joaquin Valley. Most of the newer districts were located in water-deficit areas. And, as pointed out above, the more recently incorporated districts tend toward the assumption of general

Table 1-6

PROPERTY QUALIFICATION FOR ELECTORS IN DISTRICTS

1880-1949 and 1950-70

Years	Number of Districts Formed	Districts with Property Qualification a	Percentage
1880-1949	214	24	11.2
1950-70	610	155	25.4

a. Does not include two Water Conservation Districts with property qualification for which dates of incorporation are not available. Districts requiring property qualification include all of the Reclamation, California Water, Water Conservation, and Water Storage Districts and three of the four Municipal Improvement Districts.

governmental responsibilities, toward a restricted franchise (with property ownership increasingly the basis for both district formation and for voting at bond and governing body elections), and toward urban and combined urban-irrigation uses (with no more than a few exclusively irrigation-use districts being established in recent decades). A greater proportion of the districts formed in the southern regions after 1950 share the latter characteristics. The general profile of geographic development is indicated by Table 1-7. Half a century ago most of the districts were tied closely to agrarian purpose and were located primarily in northern California. Voting for representatives on governing bodies was, in the main, open to registered, resident electors. The newer districts, found in the southern regions of the state, differ markedly in purpose and in governing style from those formed earlier in the north.

Legislative sanction was given certain classes of districts for the capture and delivery of water beyond the limits of territory included in the formation of the district, and nearly all of the authorizing legislation made it possible for districts to engage in activities not related to water use. A few of the classes of districts responsible for water utility functions are virtually indistinguishable from general governments. Thus, in 1971, 16 of the Community Services Districts

Table 1-7

INCORPORATION OF DISTRICTS BY GEOGRAPHIC SETTING, 1880-1970

	1880-89		1890-99		1900-09		1910-19		1920-29		1930-39		1940-49		1950-59		1960-69		1970-	
	No.	%	No.	%	No.	%	No.	%	No.	%	No.	%	No.	%	No.	%	No.	%	No.	%
Sacramento Valley Butte, Colusa, Glenn, Sacramento, Solano, Sutter, Tehama, Yolo, Yuba counties	8	60	0	0	1	50	11	37	10	13	3	9	5	7	29	10	26	9	1	2
San Joaquin Valley Fresno, Kern, Kings, Madera, Merced, San Joaquin, Stanislaus, Tulare counties	1	40	0	0	1	50	8	27	26	35	12	38	20	29	98	35	63	22	17	40
Central Coastal Alameda, Contra Costa, Lake, Marin, Monterey, Napa, San Benito, San Francisco, San Luis Obispo, San Mateo, Santa Clara, Santa Cruz, Sonoma counties	0	0	0	0	0	0	3	10	3	4	2	6	12	17	30	11	46	16	1	2
Northern Coastal and Mountain Del Norte, Humboldt, Mendocino, Shasta, Siskiyou, Trinity, Lassen, Modoc, Plumas counties	0	0	0	0	0	0	2	7	8	11	1	3	6	9	21	7	36	13	6	14

Table 1-7 (Cont.)

INCORPORATION OF DISTRICTS BY GEOGRAPHIC SETTING, 1880-1970

	1880-89 No.	%	1890-99 No.	%	1900-09 No.	%	1910-19 No.	%	1920-29 No.	%	1930-39 No.	%	1940-49 No.	%	1950-59 No.	%	1960-69 No.	%	1970- No.	%
Eastern Mountain Alpine, Amador, Calaveras, El Dorado, Inyo, Mariposa, Mono, Nevada, Placer, Sierra, Tuolumne Counties	0	0	0	0	0	0	0	0	2	3	3	9	18	26	17	6	36	13	2	5
Southern California Imperial, Los Angeles, Orange, Riverside, San Bernardino, San Diego, Santa Barbara, Ventura counties	0	0	1	100	0	0	6	20	26	35	11	34	8	12	88	31	78	27	15	36

provided fire protection, 28 were active in waste disposal, 8 maintained recreation and park programs, 21 were responsible for lighting and lighting maintenance, 2 supplied library services, 1 had local and regional planning responsibilities, 2 provided police protection, 8 constructed and maintained streets and roads, and 1 supplied ambulance service. The types of activities performed in 1970-71 by the 886 districts are shown in Table 1-8. That table lists only those authorized activities actually undertaken which involved financial transactions during the fiscal year; it is not suggestive of the range of activity likely to be generated by the districts. Activities in districts of the California Water and Water Storage types are to date concentrated strongly on water utility functions. Large-scale corporate agriculture is a characteristic of such districts; there are farm operations but few farm settlers and few communities.

WATER DISTRICTS AND INDICATORS OF CITIZEN INVOLVEMENT

When classified by type of governing body, three categories of district are produced. One category includes those districts governed by directors elected according to a one person/one vote electoral system. Examples of this type are Public Utility Districts, Irrigation Districts, and County Water Districts. A second type is governed by directors who are elected by a property-weighted system of voting. Water Storage Districts and California Water Districts are examples of such property qualification districts. In the third category, directors are appointed by the respective county board of supervisors. Districts whose directors are appointed by the county board of supervisors include Harbors and Ports, Maintenance Districts, and County Service Areas. The Metropolitan Water District, whose directors are appointed by the chief executive officers of constituent municipalities and districts, is listed in this category.

Our indicators of voter participation and of political competition are based on analysis of the 1967-71 and 1973-75 elections. We have calculated the turnout proportion for the various categories of districts as well as the number of elections held. We have also calculated the proportion of contested seats on district boards, the number of candidates for each position, and the proportion of

Table 1-8

ACTIVITIES NOT DIRECTLY RELATED TO WATER USE ENGAGED IN BY DISTRICTS CONDUCTING WATER UTILITY OPERATIONS, 1970-71

Activity a/ and Number of Districts of Each Type Reporting the Activity

Type of District	1	2	3	4	5	6	7	8	9	10	11	12	13	14	15
COMMUNITY SERVICES	16	28		8				21	2		1	2	8	1	103
FLOOD CONTROL AND W.C.				1	5										7
HARBOR AND PORTS															1
MUNICIPAL IMPROVEMENT	3	4		1	1			2		1		2	2		4
MAINTENANCE		6						6							33
RECLAMATION							3								8
RECREATION AND PARKS	1	5	1	1											6
COUNTY SERVICE AREAS	1	3		1	3			3				1	3		28
MUNICIPAL UTILITY		2													3
PUBLIC UTILITY	8	25	2	5	1			6							52
CALIFORNIA WATER		7		1	1										160
COUNTY WATER	7	38		2	1	1		1							192
METROPOLITAN WATER															1
MUNICIPAL WATER	1	7	3												50
WATER AGENCY				1	1	2									24
WATER CONSERVATION															8
WATER REPLENISHMENT															1
WATER STORAGE															8
COUNTY WATERWORKS		5		1											90
IRRIGATION		2	8	6											107
	37	132	12	31	7	8	3	39	2	1	1	5	13	1	886

a/ Key to Activities

    1-Fire Protection
    2-Waste Disposal
    3-Electric Utility
    4-Recreation and Parks
    5-Drainage
    6-Flood Control and Water Conservation
    7-Levee Maintenance and Land Reclamation
    8-Lighting and Lighting Maintenance
    9-Library Services
    10-Parking
    11-Local and Regional Planning
    12-Police Protection and Personal Safety
    13-Streets and Roads, Construction and Maintenance
    14-Ambulance Service
    15-Water Utility Operations

Source: State Controller, Annual Report of Financial Transactions Concerning Special Districts of California (Other Than Water Utility) Fiscal Year 1970-71.

appointed or uncontested elections. These indicators identify the districts which seem to encourage citizen participation in the electoral process and those districts which appear to discourage participation. Not surprisingly, one person/one vote districts produce greater voter participation and more competitive politics than do the property qualification districts.

Where the enabling legislation prescribes elections of directors, such elections are contested only infrequently and many directors are appointed rather than elected. When an election is held only a modest voter turnout is recorded. Where property-weighted electoral systems are employed, relatively more directors are appointed and even lower voter turnout is experienced on those few occasions when elections are actually held. These are the conclusions of the earlier study of 1,383 elections held in the years 1967-71 in 614 water districts.[3] That study showed that from 1967-71 only 375 elections were contested, while on 1,008 occasions the directorships were filled by appointment. During that period water districts therefore held elections only 27 percent of the time. The four types of districts which require property-weighted elections experienced even lower election rates; the rate during 1967-71 for elections in districts authorized by the California Water District Act being, for example, only 6 percent. For all property-weighted districts no more than 16 percent held elections during 1967-71. We have extended our survey of water district elections into 1973 and 1975.

Our data for water district elections in 1973 and 1975 confirm the findings of the study of elections in the 1967-71 period. Our tabulations show that in 1973 districts reported 558 directorships available for contest, and 1,681 in 1975 (Table 1-9). In 1973 elections were held 21.8 percent of the time; in 1975 the rate rose to 29.7 percent. It should be borne in mind that these percentages are probably high; many districts do not file reports with the Secretary of State and it is likely that the great majority of such districts did not hold elections.

We have computed average voter turnout in contested elections, by type of district, for both 1973 and 1975. The one person/one vote districts score relatively high. Public Utility Districts averaged 46.6 percent in 1975 (93 elections) and 45.4 percent in 1973 (28 elections), Irrigation Districts attained 29 percent in 1975 (21 elections) and 40.1 percent in 1973 (6 elections). Few elections were held in property-weighted districts and it is not easy to determine voter

Table 1-9

ELECTIONS OF WATER DISTRICT DIRECTORS, BY TYPE OF DISTRICT, 1973 and 1975

	1973			1975		
	Number of seats Available	Seats by Election; %	(No.)	Number of seats Available	Seats by Election; %	(No.)
Community Service	110	16.	(18)	342	37.	(128)
Public Utility	31	29.	(9)	89	44.	(39)
County Water	158	47.	(74)	549	38.	(207)
Water Agency/Authority	4	50.	(2)	35	23.	(8)
Water Conservation[b]	--	--		27	11.	
Irrigation	64	28.	(18)	222	18.	(40)
Municipal Water	1	100.	(1)	--	--	
Municipal Improvement[c]	--	--		10	50.	(5)
County Water Works	--	--		5	0.0	(0)
Recreation & Parks	6	0.0	(0)	72	35.	(25)
Water Storage[a]	28	0.0	(0)	28	0.07	(2)
Reclamation[a]	--	--		21	0.0	(0)
California Water[a]	156	0.0	(0)	281	5.	(43)
	558	21.8		1,681	29.7	(500)

a. Property-weighted electoral systems only
b. Includes two property-weighted electoral system districts
c. Includes three property-weighted electoral system districts

turnout. Certificates, when they are available, show only the total number of votes and not the number of voters; therefore we have no precise measure of voter turnout in such districts but are confident that the turnout in property-weighted districts did not exceed 5 percent in 1975. In 1973 we have no record of an election in a property qualification district. In summary we find that one person/one vote districts conduct more elections and produce a higher voter turnout when elections are held than do districts which use property qualification systems. And for one person/one vote districts, participation tends to decline as population density increases. But participation levels in property qualification districts are unaffected by variation in rural or urban settings.

We have already cited the four major enabling acts which are employed by landowners to establish districts with property qualifications for voting. The act with the greatest present appeal is the California Water District Act (Water Code 3400 et seq). As shown in Tables 1-5 and 1-6, in the decade 1950–59, 69 California Water Districts were formed. In the succeeding decade, 1960–69, 72 were incorporated. California Water Districts are formed by petition of property owners and can perform many significant services. It is worth noting what services such districts can perform. They can, for example, construct and maintain project works for irrigation, domestic, industrial, and municipal purposes. They may acquire and construct necessary facilities to provide sewer service. They also can issue both general obligation and revenue bonds and bring eminent domain proceedings to purchase and condemn property for district purposes. Finally, this type of district may form any number of special improvement districts within its boundaries and issue bonds to finance improvements within these "minidistricts." These special improvement districts, incidentally, are governed by the same board that governs the parent district. With this vast array of powers and the resulting impact these districts can have on their residents, it is interesting to note that participation in elections is restricted to property owners who may cast one vote for each dollar's worth of land to which they hold title as shown on the district's assessment roll. Voters may vote in person or by proxy. Members of the governing board need not be residents. Districts may be divided into separate wards or divisions for the purpose of electing directors. Owners of property constitute the electorate not only on questions of district formation and representation on the board of directors but also on the incurring of bonded indebtedness. It is not surprising that this type of district is popular with landowners, especially landowners with large holdings. The California Water District Act gives these individuals or corporations a variety of options and considerable political influence. In the Westlands Water District, for example, a district which comprises 597,778 acres and has more than 3,000 landowners, 10 landowners account for 43 percent of all the land in the district. This situation, coupled with assessed valuation voting, means that a handful or so of corporations and individuals effectively controls district elections. Nominating petitions for the 1971 board elections in Westlands indicate how trusts and corporations relate to political influence. In that year, according to the information on nominating petitions on file in the Fresno County Elections Department, a current board of directors member signed a nominating petition in the following manner: in his own name; as vice president of one corporation; as president of another; and as trustee of a children's trust.[4]

We think it instructive to note the year-by-year electoral performance of all districts which are authorized by a property-qualification enabling act, the Water Storage District Act. Tables 1-10, 1-11, and 1-12 report the number of uncontested and contested elections, with the number of available seats and number of candidates, in each of the eight water storage districts of Kern and Kings counties from 1965-75. During that period, there were contests in 16 of 162 elections and a low seat-to-candidate ratio of 1 to 1.05.

In some property-test districts a clear majority of the votes cast is at the disposal of no more than four or five landowners; Westlands is such a district. In others, a single owner can cast the majority of all votes; Tulare Lake Basin Water Storage District in the large-scale farming areas of the southern San Joaquin Valley, and the Irvine Ranch Water District in once agricultural but now rapidly urbanizing Orange County are examples. In the Tulare Lake Basin Water Storage District, four corporations farm nearly 85 percent of the district's land, and J. G. Boswell Corporation alone, with its vast landholdings, commands 37,845 votes, enough to determine who is elected to the district board of directors. One hundred and eighty-nine landowners own 80 acres or less and their holdings aggregate only 2.34 percent of the agricultural acreage in the district. The Irvine Company is the dominant influence in the Irvine Ranch Water District, a California Water District. When the district was formed in 1961, the Irvine Company owned 38,750 acres; the remaining 750 acres were held by 31 different owners. In many other districts, our data show a strong trend toward a more consolidated ownership of land. Berrenda Mesa Water District, a California Water District in the southern San Joaquin, exemplifies that trend. Districts which set property tests for voting tend to be incorporated in areas where relatively large-scale farming is the

Table 1-10

ELECTIONS IN WATER STORAGE DISTRICTS, 1973 and 1975;
NUMBER OF UNCONTESTED AND CONTESTED ELECTIONS
AND NUMBER OF AVAILABLE SEATS AND CANDIDATES

1975

Name of District	Uncontested	Contested	No. of Seats	No. of Candidates	Division
Arvin Edison	X		5	5	2,4,6,8,9
Belridge	X		3	3	2,3,5
Buena Vista	X		2	2	2,4
North Kern	X		2	2	2,5
Rosedale - Rio Bravo	1 seat Div. 5	X	3	5	1,4 contested
Semitropic	X		4	4	1,3,4,6
Tulare Lake Basin	X		5	5	2,4,6,7,11
Wheeler Ridge Mariposa	X		4	4	2,4,5,9

1973

Name of District	Uncontested	Contested	No. of Seats	No. of Candidates	Division
Arvin Edison	X		4	4	1,3,5,7
Belridge	X		2	2	1,4
Buena Vista	X		3	3	1,3,5
North Kern	X		3	3	1,3,4
Rosedale Rio Bravo	X		2	2	2,3
Smitropic	X		3	3	2,5,7
Tulare Lake Basin	X		6	6	1,3,5,8,9,10
Wheeler Ridge Mariposa	X		5	5	1,3,6,7,8

Table 1-11

ELECTIONS IN WATER STORAGE DISTRICTS, 1969 and 1971:
NUMBER OF UNCONTESTED AND CONTESTED ELECTIONS
AND NUMBER OF AVAILABLE SEATS AND CANDIDATES

1971

Name of District	Uncontested	Contested	No. of Seats	No. of Candidates	Division
Arvin Edison	X		5	5	2,4,6,8,9
Belridge	X		3	3	2,3,5
Buena Vista	X		2	2	2,4
North Kern	X		2	2	2,5
Rosedale - Rio Bravo	X		3	3	1,4,5
Semitropic	X		4	4	1,3,4,6
Tulare Lake Basin	X		5	5	2,4,6,7,11
Wheeler Ridge Mariposa	X		4	4	2,4,5,9

1969

Name of District	Uncontested	Contested	No. of Seats	No. of Candidates	Division
Arvin Edison	X		4	4	1,3,5,7
Belridge	X		2	2	1,4
Buena Vista	X		3	3	1,3,5
North Kern	X		3	3	1,3,4
Rosedale-Rio Bravo	X Div. 3	X	2	3	2
Semitropic	X		3	3	2,5,7
Tulare Lake Basin	No Election or Appointments				
Wheeler Ridge Mariposa	X	X Div. 1	5	6	1 contested 3,6,7,8 app.

Table 1-12

ELECTIONS IN WATER STORAGE DISTRICTS, 1965 and 1967:
NUMBER OF UNCONTESTED AND CONTESTED ELECTIONS
AND NUMBER OF AVAILABLE SEATS AND CANDIDATES

Name of District	Uncontested	Contested	No. of Seats	No. of Candidates	Division
1967					
Arvin Edison	X		5	5	2,4,6,8,9
Belridge	X		3	3	2,3,5
Buena Vista	X		2	2	2,4
North Kern	X		2	2	2,5
Rosedale - Rio Bravo	X		3	3	1,4,5
Semitropic	X		4	4	1,3,4,6
*Tulare Lake Basin		X	11	15	11 contested
Wheeler Ridge Mariposa	X	X	4	5	1 contested 4,5,9 app.
1965					
Arvin Edison	X		4	4	1,3,5,7
Belridge	X		2	2	1,4
Buena Vista	X		3	3	1,3,5
North Kern	X		3	3	1,3,4
Rosedale-Rio Bravo	X		2	2	2,3
Semitropic	X		3	3	2,5,7
Tulare Lake Basin	No Election or Election Appointments				
Wheeler Ridge Mariposa	X		5	5	1,3,6,7,8

* Special election May 23, 1967

norm. Property qualification districts and extensive corporate agriculture cluster in the southern and western San Joaquin.[5]

Seventeen landowners in the Berrenda Mesa district presently own more than 500 acres each and their holdings account for 87.8 percent of the district. Table 1-13 lists the holdings of the major landowners and their votes. Blackwell Land Company, Inc., owned by a group of international corporations, is the district's largest landowner and taxpayer and controls the largest amount of votes. Blackwell Land Company owns 15,355 acres, 27.8 percent of the total assessable acreage. Its affiliate, Blackwell Management Company, acts as manager for Blackwell Land and an additional 4,978 acres in the district is leased by it from non-Blackwell owners. Berrenda Mesa Farming Company, direct owner of 940 acres, also acts as farm manager for 30 additional owners. Berrenda Mesa Farming Company manages about 14,000 acres in the Berrenda Mesa Water District, 4,000 acres in adjacent property qualification water districts, and 2,000 acres in other areas. Voting is determined by one vote per each $100.00 of assessed valuation of land owned. Since proxy voting is allowed, it is possible that Blackwell Land and Berrenda Mesa Farms control the majority of votes in the district. Our records show a steady increase in the number of farms owned by corporations and a steady decline in the number of farms owned by individuals. Table 1-14 illustrates the movement toward corporate agriculture in the Berrenda Mesa Water District for a four-year period, 1973-76.

DISTRICTS BY GEOGRAPHIC LOCALE

We have already noted the regional distribution of types of district. Our statistical analysis compares regional areas and we identify districts as (1) urban, (2) suburban, and (3) rural. Using the criteria and data of the *County and City Data Book, 1975*[6] we divided the 58 counties of California into three exclusive categories. "Urban" counties are those counties where over 70 percent of the population resides in urban areas. "Suburban" counties have upper and lower bounds of 70 percent and 30 percent respectively, and "rural" counties are those where under 30 percent of the population resides in urban areas. Appendix A lists the counties by category. Our statistical analysis also compares the performance of districts by

Table 1-13

BERRENDA MESA WATER DISTRICT; LANDOWNERS WITH
HOLDINGS EXCEEDING 500 ACRES, 1976

OWNER	ACREAGE	NO. OF VOTES
Blackwell Land	15,355[a]	767,750
Getty Oil	4,659	232,950
E.M. Still Estate	4,500	225,000
JB2H	4,050	202,500
Mendiburu	3,733	186,650
Westside Ranch IV	3,291	164,550
El Vic Farm Corp.	2,985	149,250
Shell Oil	2,232	111,600
JHRD III Inc.	1,677	83,850
Flavy Davis	1,120	56,000
Berrenda Mesa Farms	940[b]	47,000
Table Top	849	42,450
Santa Maria	720	36,000
Lucky Tree	691	34,550
Midori	687	31,850
St. Vincent	600	30,000
Stephans	506	25,300
Total (17 owners)	48,545	2,427,250
Balance of Assessable acres	6,729	336,450
Total Assessable acres (85 owners)	55,274	2,763,700

a. Blackwell leases and manages 4,978 additional acres.
b. Berrenda Mesa Farms leases and manages over 14,000 additional acres.
SOURCE: Berrenda MWD Tax rolls

Table 1-14

BERRENDA MESA WATER DISTRICT: TYPE
OF LANDOWNER, 1973-76

Type of Owner*	No.	(Percent) 1973	No.	(Percent) 1974	No.	(Percent) 1975	No.	(Percent) 1976
CORPORATIONS	26	(35)	36	(41.8)	39	(45.9)	45	(55.6)
INDIVIDUALS	32	(43.2)	31	(36.1)	29	(34.1)	24	(29.6)
PARTNERSHIPS	12	(16.2)	14	(16.2)	11	(12.9)	10	(12.3)
ESTATES	2	(2.7)	2	(2.3)	3	(3.5)	0	(0)
TRUSTS	2	(2.7)	3	(3.5)	3	(3.5)	3	(2.5)
TOTALS	74	(100.0)	86	(100.0)	85	(100.0)	81	(100.0)

Source: Berrenda Mesa Water District "Summary of all Taxes, 1973-76, by Land Owner."

* Classification of ownership type by the authors. Owners listed as companies and/or with fictitious names were considered corporations even though this might not always be the case. Trusts include non-profit institutions.

service area; districts in federal service areas and districts in state service areas are compared.

OUR CLASSIFICATION SCHEME SUMMARIZED

Our review of state enabling legislation yielded 20 categories of water districts. When classified by type of governing body, three categories were produced. These categories include districts governed by directors elected according to a one person/one vote system, districts whose directors are elected by a property-weighted system, and districts whose directors are appointed by a county board of supervisors. Our analysis of citizen involvement drew attention to two classes of district; these are the one person/one vote districts and, secondly, property-qualification districts. Our survey of geographic locale classified districts as either urban, suburban, or rural. Finally, we sorted water districts into two additional geographically determined categories, those in federal service areas and those in state service areas. These are the principal types of water districts whose capabilities we measured.[7]

NOTES

1. This section is based on a chapter prepared by Goodall, "Authorizing and Empowering Water Districts in California," in Jamieson, Hirsch, Sonenblum, Goodall, and others, *Some Political and Economic Aspects of Managing California Water Districts* (Los Angeles: Institute of Government and Public Affairs, 1974), pp. 9–48. Permission to reproduce these materials has been granted by the University of California at Los Angeles.

2. Samuel E. Wood and Alfred E. Heller, *The Phantom Cities of California* (Sacramento: California Tomorrow, 1963), p. 44.

3. See *Some Political and Economic Aspects of Managing California Water Districts*, pp. 154–185.

4. This paragraph is drawn from Goodall and Jamieson, "Property Qualification Voting in Rural California's Water Districts," *Land Economics* (August 1974), p. 293.

5. But the beginnings of such agriculture were apparent in the 1930s and before. See Goodall, "Land and Power Administration in the Central Valley," *Journal of Land and Public Utility Economics* (August 1942), pp. 299–311.

6. U.S. Bureau of the Census, *County and City Data Book, 1975* (Washington, D.C.: U.S. Government Printing Office, 1975).

7. For a discussion of our major methods of comparison see the methodological note in Appendix B.

CHAPTER
2

Patterns of Financial Performance: General Description and Trends

THE USE OF STATE CONTROLLER DATA: RELEVANCE AND LIMITATIONS

Special districts in California are required by law to submit annual budgetary and other descriptive data to the State Controller. Few efforts have ever been made to tap this potentially valuable source of information. Until very recently, the State Controller did not retain the raw data tapes used in preparing the annual report. Our analysis by computer of these data therefore represents a unique social science exercise. In the following section, we present a summary of findings based on Controller Report data from the years 1960–70.

However, there are some limitations and inescapable problems. There are variations in reporting behavior by certain types of special districts. A prior analysis of the Controller data appears in our statement to the Westland hearings, where we observed a significant difference between selected property qualification districts and popularly elected districts in measures of reporting behavior, range of variation, and rates of return for expenditures.[1] Until 1967, for example, the property qualification California Water Districts typically failed to report complete and accurate data.

As many as 85 percent of all California Water Districts failed in a single year to report their financial transactions to the Controller of the State of California; no more than 22 percent of the one person/one vote Irrigation Districts failed to report their financial data. In Table 2-1 we compare the varying willingness of Irrigation Districts and California Water Districts to meet this statutory requirement. This in itself is a finding of some significance. Missing information is somewhat common and may bias our findings to some extent.

Table 2-1

FREQUENCY OF FINANCIAL REPORTING TO THE STATE CONTROLLER:
IRRIGATION DISTRICTS AND CALIFORNIA WATER DISTRICTS

	IRRIGATION DISTRICTS			CALIFORNIA WATER DISTRICTS		
YEAR	No. of Districts	No. Reporting	Percentage Reporting	No. of Districts	No. Reporting	Percentage Reporting
1960–61	108	100	93	76	11	15
1964–65	104	92	88.5	109	77	71
1967–68	105	94	99.5	114	87	77
1968–69	96	76	79	99	37	58
1970–71	95	73	78	99	37	58

A second limitation which confounds simple interpretation results from a change of format of reporting forms instituted by the Controller's office in 1968. For example, after 1967 revenues were divided into operating and non-operating categories. In the tables that follow, trends are discernible for two sets of time points. The first includes 1960–61, 1964–65, and 1967–68, whereas the second includes 1968–69 and 1970–71 unless otherwise noted.

The proper utilization of the Controller data has just begun. Our study represents an initial effort to present aggregated measures of central tendency. We also propose indices of fiscal performance. These measures tell us about typical performance scores and typical variations within groups over time and significant differences in performance according to variations in population density, geographic location, and type of enabling legislation. In effect, we ask the following kinds of questions:

What is a typical revenue-expenditure ration for x type of districts?
Which districts show the greatest uniformity in performance?
How do different types of districts vary over time and between each other?
What are the sources of revenue financing for different types of districts?
What effect does population density have on fiscal performance measures?

In sum, then, this and the following chapter attempt to establish standards of performance by which one can evaluate the performance of individual districts and/or individual types of districts. The data below are reflective of typical performance. Much remains to be done in terms of delineating and defining factors such as age of the district, the geographic locale, and the source of water supply that cause deviations from these norms.

We are concerned initially with some basic patterns of financial performance. As we noted earlier, our interest here is focused in part on the districts grouped by the three types of decision system—one person/one vote, property qualification, and county board appointed. We also have the data grouped by type of enabling act and, from time to time, we will present appropriate comparisons of enabling acts. Furthermore, it should be noted that the amount of data analyzed by the project is very extensive and that we have had to select variables for presentation. The tables that follow in this and the next section tend to be typical of the many relationships we examined. One final point needs to be made—in this section, we present a discussion and series of tables which are primarily descriptive in character and are intended to convey to the reader some of the dimensions of water districts in California. This is done by describing districts by type of enabling act and by type of political system. In our next section, we turn to more analytical concerns and explore a variety of relationships between many of our variables.

ACREAGE (Table 2-2)

Let us begin our examination of water districts with a look at the physical base from which the various types of districts operate. Table 2-2 presents average acreage in each type of district.[2] In cases where no acreage is recorded the Controller's report did not contain this information in that year. Some interesting comparisons can be made in this table. First, note that the average acreage for Irrigation Districts has remained quite stable over the 10-year period covered by the data. The average district has increased in size by only approximately 4,000 acres. This represents the contrast between a type of district, Irrigation, which is used less in recent years as a mechanism to create water delivery systems, with California Water Districts, which have tended to become a preferred mode of performing water utility functions during this time period. One other matter to note in the table is the size of the Metropolitan Water District in southern California. This particular district is a unique type. Its uniqueness is reflected in the manner by which members of the Board of Directors of the district are chosen, as we have noted.[3]

In terms of the average size of districts, it is interesting to note that in some instances the number of districts has increased even though the average size of districts has decreased. For instance, the number of Public Utility Districts has increased from 9 to 41, while the average size of these districts has declined by about 10,000 acres. This suggests that a number of smaller districts have been formed under this enabling act in recent years.

DISTRICT REVENUES (Table 2-3)

In Table 2-3, we present total revenues for all types of districts for the period 1960–71. As we noted above, the Controller's office changed its mode of reporting in 1968–69 and this has caused some discontinuities in this and subsequent tables. Both revenues and expenditures were subdivided into operating and non-operating

Patterns of Financial Performance: General Description 33

categories. Our figures represent the "operating" figures. As this table indicates, water district revenues have increased over this time period almost without exception. Some comparisons are worth noting. First, many of the types of districts exhibit considerable stability over this time period. Irrigation Districts, for instance, show a steady increase in revenues up to 1967–68, when reporting procedures changed, and a similar steady increase in the latter two years. This pattern holds for most of the district types, with some exceptions. California Water Districts, for example, show an *wrong.* increase up to 1968–69 and then a rather sharp drop. This could be due to the fact that three California districts were created that year and it is possible that they had not yet started operations, thus depressing the average. In general, however, the pattern exhibited is one of a steady increase in revenues.

REVENUES FROM LEVIES (Table 2-4)

Table 2-4 presents, for all types of districts, the amount of revenue derived from levy assessments. In general, this trend has been for the amount of revenue derived from levy assessments to increase over this 11-year period. Some districts such as Community Services exhibited considerable stability while others, such as California Water, exhibited considerable growth in the amount of revenue derived from levy assessments.

RATES OF LEVY (Table 2-5)

Turning to the question of average rates of levy per $100.00 of assessed valuation, we can see from Table 2-5 that most districts were extremely stable in terms of such rates. Most district types have lower rates—under $5.00 per $100.00 of assessed valuation. There were no abrupt discontinuities in levy rates. Two exceptions are Water Storage Districts which went from a low of $0.698 to a high of $8.84 (see also Table 3-19).

Table 2-2

AVERAGE ACREAGE BY TYPE OF DISTRICT

	1960-61	1964-65	1967-68	1968-69	1970-71
IRR	41437.327 (110)	42907.280 (107)	44097.019 (108)	45544.573 (103)	45680.942 (103)
CSA	0.000 (1)	0.000 (1)	0.000 (10)	894.500 (2)	7373.000 (4)
MTR	---	---	---	2061760.000 (1)	3064600.000 (134)
CAL	0.000 (6)	1427.143 (7)	0.000 (7)	15244.746 (122)	14433.896 (134)
MIM	---	---	---	---	1375.000 (1)
CMS	0.000 (1)	0.000 (1)	0.000 (1)	3935.800 (10)	4633.952 (62)
CWT	---	---	---	20495.932 (162)	22800.253 (186)
FCN	---	---	---	516837.688 (3)	410666.000 (6)
MNT	---	0.000 (1)	---	---	143.231 (26)
HPT	---	---	---	---	---
RCP	---	0.000 (1)	0.000 (1)	---	1870.375 (8)
RCM	---	---	---	---	23326.000 (1)
MUT	---	---	---	---	17813.000 (1)
PUT	---	---	---	23492.788 (9)	13322.317 (41)

Table 2-2 (Cont.)

AVERAGE ACREAGE BY TYPE OF DISTRICT

	1960-61	1964-65	1967-68	1968-69	1970-71
REP	—	—	—	—	80.000 (1)
STR	—	—	—	412.000 (1)	420.667 (6)
CNV	—	—	—	83083.000 (7)	58381.300 (10)
MWT	0.000 (1)	0.000 (1)	0.000 (1)	75161.488 (41)	74606.737 (42)
CWK	0.000 (1)	0.000 (2)	0.000 (1)	8741.432 (88)	7673.337 (92)
WAG	—	—	—	383412.212 (16)	406083.801 (20)

Table 2-3

AVERAGE DISTRICT REVENUES BY TYPE OF DISTRICT

	1960-61	1964-65	1967-68	1968-69	1970-71
IRR	462.074 (108)	609.115 (104)	642.914 (105)	264.554 (101)	292.693 (101)
CSA	16.500 (2)	83.333 (3)	279.500 (4)	30.500 (2)	59.750 (4)
MTR	24924.000 (1)	51717.000 (1)	63053.000 (1)	38334.000 (1)	47140.000 (1)
CAL	51.605 (76)	90.752 (109)	99.130 (115)	223.071 (113)	88.000 (116)
MIM	61.000 (2)	485.500 (2)	557.500 (2)	--	175.000 (4)
CMS	38.341 (32)	52.628 (113)	61.611 (113)	61.923 (13)	192.194 (67)
CWT	135.493 (146)	234.253 (158)	285.510 (151)	272.311 (183)	189.163 (184)
FCN	1430.667 (30)	2164.107 (28)	3229.821 (28)	4021.000 (3)	1104.286 (7)
MNT	12.818 (11)	5.864 (44)	12.938 (32)	--	0.741 (27)
HPT	87.000 (1)	164.000 (1)	178.000 (1)	14.000 (1)	14.000 (1)
RCP	--	32.333 (12)	68.167 (18)	--	8.125 (8)
RCM	697.000 (1)	741.000 (1)	877.000 (1)	--	232.000 (1)
MUT	334.000 (3)	342.333 (3)	395.333 (3)	19.000 (1)	44.000 (3)
PUT	700.282 (39)	731.818 (48)	859.938 (48)	66.833 (12)	675.143 (42)

Table 2-3 (Cont.)

AVERAGE DISTRICT REVENUES BY TYPE OF DISTRICT

	1960-61	1964-65	1967-68	1968-69	1970-71
REP	—	—	—	—	0.000 (1)
STR	35.167 (6)	43.500 (6)	53.500 (6)	7.000 (1)	22.571 (7)
CNV	160.100 (10)	304.091 (11)	406.000 (11)	346.500 (8)	398.200 (10)
MWT	384.886 (44)	713.244 (45)	905.356 (45)	745.927 (41)	984.372 (43)
CWK	54.103 (87)	95.322 (90)	105.708 (89)	70.191 (94)	98.777 (94)
WAG	169.867 (15)	483.353 (17)	798.944 (18)	315.800 (20)	362.850 (20)

Table 2-4

AVERAGE REVENUES FROM LEVIES BY TYPE OF DISTRICT

	1960-61	1964-65	1967-68	1968-69	1970-71
IRR	99.130 (108)	109.529 (104)	111.495 (105)	135.515 (101)	140.119 (101)
CSA	16.500 (2)	67.667 (3)	146.000 (4)	38.750 (4)	0.000 (2)
MTR	8266.000 (1)	10850.000 (1)	23089.000 (1)	46756.000 (1)	55716.000 (1)
CAL	9.000 (76)	10.422 (109)	26.380 (100)	31.970 (101)	47.327 (101)
MIM	15.500 (2)	203.500 (2)	243.000 (2)	—	—
CMS	10.071 (84)	13.044 (113)	19.053 (113)	11.769 (13)	11.909 (66)
CWT	16.596 (146)	38.481 (158)	49.559 (152)	63.415 (183)	67.460 (187)
FCN	952.300 (30)	1512.143 (28)	1939.536 (28)	418.333 (3)	348.000 (7)
MNT	14.100 (10)	6.545 (44)	11.094 (32)	—	7.148 (27)
HPT	50.000 (1)	102.000 (1)	104.000 (1)	0.000 (1)	0.000 (1)
RCP	—	28.750 (12)	44.278 (18)	—	25.500 (8)
RECM	0.000 (1)	0.000 (1)	10.000 (1)	—	0.000 (1)
MUT	247.667 (3)	245.667 (3)	296.000 (3)	0.000 (1)	38.364 (11)
PUT	121.975 (40)	121.298 (47)	130.208 (48)	38.364 (11)	127.667 (42)

Table 2-4 (Cont.)

AVERAGE REVENUES FROM LEVIES BY TYPE OF DISTRICT

	1960-61	1964-65	1967-68	1968-69	1970-71
REP	--	--	--	--	0.000 (1)
STR	11.000 (6)	14.333 (6)	17.500 (6)	3.000 (1)	3.571 (7)
CNV	151.400 (10)	72.182 (11)	85.091 (11)	226.375 (8)	73.500 (10)
MWT	65.841 (44)	120.622 (45)	136.444 (45)	209.561 (41)	294.442 (43)
CWK	16.793 (87)	18.056 (90)	22.270 (89)	61.426 (94)	71.191 (94)
WAG	76.600 (15)	175.176 (17)	284.278 (18)	383.100 (20)	343.650 (20)

Table 2-5

AVERAGE RATES OF LEVY BY TYPE OF DISTRICT

	1960-61	1964-65	1967-68	1968-69	1970-71
IRR	2.622 (103)	3.890 (104)	2.652 (105)	2.971 (96)	3.046 (95)
CSA	333.143 (3)	0.000 (3)	0.000 (4)	0.000 (2)	0.000 (4)
MTR	0.060 (1)	0.060 (1)	0.100 (1)	0.160 (1)	0.170 (1)
CAL	1.194 (76)	0.698 (109)	0.816 (114)	1.128 (99)	—
MIM	0.000 (2)	1.250 (2)	1.850 (2)	—	1.340 (2)
CMS	0.509 (83)	0.517 (113)	0.621 (113)	0.462 (13)	0.625 (66)
CWT	0.356 (146)	0.674 (158)	0.530 (151)	0.793 (183)	0.918 (187)
FCN	0.084 (30)	0.074 (25)	0.018 (27)	0.022 (4)	0.099 (7)
MNT	0.765 (10)	0.376 (43)	1.006 (32)	—	0.523 (27)
HPT	0.030 (1)	0.050 (1)	0.040 (1)	0.000 (1)	0.000 (1)
RCP	—	0.123 (12)	0.324 (18)	—	1.391 (8)
RCM	0.000 (5)	0.221 (13)	0.114 (14)	—	0.000 (1)
MUT	0.167 (3)	0.317 (3)	0.450 (3)	0.000 (1)	0.000 (3)
PUT	1.070 (46)	0.932 (47)	0.891 (47)	0.535 (11)	0.685 (42)

Table 2-5 (Cont.)

AVERAGE RATES OF LEVY BY TYPE OF DISTRICT

	1960-61	1964-65	1967-68	1968-69	1970-71
REP	0.010 (1)	0.010 (1)	0.000 (1)	—	0.000 (1)
STR	4.143 (7)	0.000 (7)	0.000 (7)	1.500 (1)	0.414 (7)
CNV	0.143 (10)	0.252 (10)	0.183 (10)	0.338 (8)	0.108 (10)
MWT	0.359 (40)	0.290 (44)	0.143 (44)	0.380 (41)	0.330 (43)
CWK	0.723 (84)	0.679 (88)	0.393 (88)	1.889 (94)	1.382 (94)
WAG	0.032 (13)	0.035 (13)	0. (11)	0.139 (20)	0.213 (20)

Table 2-6

AVERAGE DEBT, TOTAL OUTSTANDING, LONGTERM

BY TYPE OF DISTRICT

	1960-61	1964-65	1967-68	1968-69	1970-71
IRR	2466.197 (108)	3490.519 (106)	3694.353 (106)	1357.970 (101)	1922.347 (101)
CSA	0.000 (2)	0.000 (3)	777.500 (4)	0.000 (2)	243.750 (4)
MTR	216671.000 (1)	238747.000 (1)	238747.000 (1)	440058.000 (1)	485649.000 (1)
CAL	173.840 (50)	611.241 (87)	741.959 (97)	876.386 (101)	950.392 (102)
MIM	847.500 (2)	18335.000 (2)	603.500 (2)	—	1404.250 (4)
CMS	176.768 (82)	161.336 (113)	160.735 (113)	265.769 (13)	186.788 (66)
CWT	1369.404 (146)	788.519 (158)	904.536 (151)	871.333 (183)	752.701 (187)
FCN	1396.867 (30)	11889.036 (28)	15355.429 (28)	12449.333 (3)	6823.000 (7)
MNT	0.000 (10)	0.000 (44)	0.000 (32)	—	0.000 (27)
HPT	0.000 (1)	157.000 (1)	54.000 (1)	0.000 (1)	0.000 (1)
RCP	—	25.167 (12)	92.556 (18)	—	137.125 (8)
RCM	0.000 (1)	0.000 (1)	0.000 (1)	—	0.000 (1)
MUT	191.000 (3)	121.667 (3)	137.667 (3)	0.000 (1)	122.000 (3)
PUT	2682.077 (39)	3903.677 (48)	3891.396 (48)	1138.364 (11)	3514.952 (42)

Table 2-6 (Cont.)

AVERAGE DEBT, TOTAL OUTSTANDING, LONGTERM
BY TYPE OF DISTRICT

	1960-61	1964-65	1967-68	1968-69	1970-71
REP	—	—	—	—	0.000 (1)
STR	180.333 (6)	172.667 (6)	214.833 (6)	27.000 (1)	46.571 (7)
CNV	118.300 (10)	1089.909 (11)	4122.636 (11)	1049.500 (8)	4503.900 (10)
MWT	1235.477 (44)	2091.644 (45)	2541.733 (45)	2372.707 (41)	3469.907 (43)
CWK	571.674 (86)	953.856 (99)	1009.256 (90)	1041.989 (94)	1089.596 (94)
WAG	40.667 (15)	6948.471 (17)	6781.556 (18)	22678.000 (20)	66484.500 (20)

Patterns of Financial Performance: General Description 43

Table 2-7

AVERAGE TOTAL EXPENDITURES BY TYPE OF DISTRICT

	1960-61	1964-65	1967-68	1968-69	1970-71
IRR	387.519 (108)	529.673 (104)	583.495 (101)	381.119 (101)	444.901 (101)
CSA	15.500 (2)	69.667 (3)	156.250 (4)	30.500 (2)	49.750 (4)
MTR	25111.000 (1)	28791.000 (1)	40953.000 (1)	2386.000 (1)	26720.000 (1)
CAL	43.079 (76)	56.000 (109)	68.405 (116)	72.018 (114)	107.581 (117)
MIM	234.500 (2)	103.000 (2)	320.500 (2)	—	97.500 (4)
CMS	32.000 (82)	41.752 (113)	45.717 (113)	40.308 (13)	43.909 (66)
CWT	101.822 (146)	218.095 (158)	246.649 (151)	149.514 (183)	185.288 (184)
FCN	1195.633 (30)	1797.857 (28)	2507.071 (28)	1569.000 (3)	932.000 (7)
MNT	12.200 (10)	4.909 (44)	13.813 (32)	—	8.444 (27)
HPT	70.000 (1)	48.000 (1)	121.000 (1)	8.000 (1)	2.000 (1)
RCP	2.000 (1)	18.727 (11)	41.167 (18)	—	20.500 (8)
RCM	566.000 (3)	692.000 (1)	820.000 (1)	—	349.000 (1)
MUT	288.000 (3)	360.000 (3)	411.000 (3)	12.000 (1)	109.333 (3)
PUT	1027.846 (39)	101.333 (48)	884.583 (48)	113.818 (11)	551.190 (42)

Table 2-7 (Cont.)

AVERAGE TOTAL EXPENDITURES BY TYPE OF DISTRICT

	1960-61	1964-65	1967-68	1968-69	1970-71
REP	—	—	—	—	0.000 (1)
STR	21.000 (6)	21.333 (6)	31.500 (6)	4.000 (1)	19.429 (7)
CNV	147.400 (10)	502.455 (11)	337.818 (11)	376.750 (8)	509.300 (10)
MWT	462.455 (44)	609.600 (45)	784.467 (45)	803.561 (41)	1251.744 (43)
CWK	280.253 (87)	139.489 (90)	90.820 (89)	95.809 (94)	116.809 (94)
WAG	188.933 (15)	280.118 (17)	528.444 (18)	220.400 (20)	290.350 (20)

TOTAL DEBT (Table 2-6)

In Table 2-6 we present the total debt by type of district and what is apparent at once is the differential in debt for different types of districts. For instance, the average debt of Irrigation Districts in 1970–71 is $1922.347, while for California Water Districts it is only $950.00. The number of districts in both cases is about the same. Similarly, Municipal Water Districts in 1970–71 incurred an average debt of $3469.907, while Water Agency Districts reached an amazing high of $66,484.550. These rather large differences may reflect the fact that different types of districts are eligible for loans from different sources (e.g., federal loans as opposed to state loans), and that interest rates will differ from source to source. In addition, they may reflect the rate at which the delivery systems in different districts are constructed. In any event, there are wide differences in terms of total debt.

TOTAL EXPENDITURE (Table 2-7)

Turning to Table 2-7, we can see that the average total expenditures for the different types of district vary somewhat but not as much as we saw in the previous table nor, as we will see, with respect to capital outlay in the next section. As the table indicates, there has been a general increase in average total expenditures over the 11-year period under study, although, in some instances, expenditures have declined. In most cases of increased expenditures, the number of existing districts has increased. On the other hand, the decline in average expenditures is accompanied with a decline of the total number of districts within that type, which would explain the decline in expenditures.

EXPENDITURES— CAPITAL OUTLAY (Table 2-8)

In contrast with general expenditures, it would appear that types of districts differ somewhat more with respect to capital expenditures.

Again, the Metropolitan Water District far exceeds all other types in this category. But an examination of this table suggests that there are rather large differences among other types as well. For instance, Irrigation, Public Utility, and Water Agencies have relatively large expenditures for capital outlay, while County Service Areas, California Water Districts, and Municipal Water Districts have rather small ones.

To this point, we have described water districts by type of enabling act and pointed to differences and similarities in these comparisons. We would now like to turn to the type of political decision system—one person/one vote, property qualification, and county board appointed—used in selecting members of the boards of directors, and to make some additional comparisons.

ACREAGE BY TYPE OF POLITICAL SYSTEM (Table 2-9)

In Table 2-9, we present average acreage by type of political decision system. As can be seen, one person/one vote districts have exhibited a fairly stable average acreage over this 10-year period, with a somewhat smaller average in the last year as opposed to earlier years. Given that the number of such districts has increased, this suggests that the newer districts may be somewhat smaller in size. The other two types of districts, on the other hand, have exhibited considerable growth. Little is known about the first three time points due to the small number of districts reporting. In the latter two time points, both property qualification and county board appointed have exhibited growth.

TOTAL REVENUE (OPERATING) (Table 2-10)

Keeping in mind the fact noted above that the State Controller changed reporting procedures in 1968, we can see that revenue for each political type increased during the first three time periods.

48 *California Water: A New Political Economy*

During the second two time periods, revenue decreased but the number of districts under each political type increased considerably. It is likely that many of these new districts were not fully operational (or not at all operational) during this time period and did not generate revenues. It is to be expected that in subsequent years, as these districts become active, revenues will increase.

REVENUE FROM ASSESSMENT LEVIES (Table 2-11)

This table is interesting in that it shows that both one person/one vote districts and county board appointed districts have tended to derive greater average amounts of revenue from levies than have the property qualification districts. This could be due to the availability of federal money for certain types of property qualification districts for which one person/one vote and county board appointed districts are not eligible. It may also have to do with the repayment schemes which property qualification districts derive for loans they obtain. We will return to this point in the summary section.

TOTAL DEBT AND EXPENDITURES (Tables 2-12 and 2-13)

Again, with respect to debt and expenditures, we observe a pattern noted earlier. The one person/one vote districts appear to exhibit considerably less oscillation than do the other two types of district. The one person/one vote districts have shown a very steady increase in expenditures and have also shown a very steady increase in debt. The property qualification districts have exhibited rather steady growth with respect to debt but have been a bit more erratic with respect to total expenditures. The same pattern can be seen with respect to the types of districts in which board members are appointed by county boards of supervisors. There have been growth trends and both debt and expenditures have exhibited ups and downs.

Table 2-8

AVERAGE EXPENDITURE - CAPITAL OUTLAY BY TYPE OF DISTRICT

	1960-61	1964-65	1967-68
IRR	65.843 (108)	97.817 (104)	119.366 (101)
CSA	1.000 (2)	2.000 (3)	9.333 (3)
MTR	11457.000 (1)	13660.000 (1)	23446.000 (1)
CAL	4.167 (60)	77.042 (95)	6.000 (2)
MIM	216.000 (2)	6.000 (2)	55.000 (2)
CMS	14.707 (82)	13.673 (113)	12.237 (114)
CWT	47.856 (146)	86.013 (159)	118.618 (152)
FCN	403.267 (30)	935.500 (28)	1124.000 (28)
MNT	0.000 (10)	0.000 (44)	0.094 (32)
HPT	33.000 (1)	9.000 (1)	76.000 (1)
RCP	0.000 (1)	6.091 (11)	12.111 (18)
RCM	51.000 (1)	116.000 (1)	209.000 (1)
MUT	8.333 (3)	21.000 (3)	22.667 (3)
PUT	672.359 (39)	27.542 (48)	553.458 (48)
REP	--	--	--
STR	6.000 (6)	3.500 (6)	7.500 (6)
CNV	9.400 (10)	175.727 (11)	20.818 (11)
MWT	152.523 (44)	104.533 (45)	91.267 (48)
CWK	37.437 (87)	14.922 (90)	26.000 (89)
WAG	68.867 (15)	57.412 (17)	300.278 (18)

Tables 2-9 through 2-13

ACREAGE TOTAL REVENUE AND REVENUE FROM LEVY ASSESSMENT
AVERAGES BY METHOD OF SELECTION OF GOVERNING BODY

	Popular		Property Qualification		Appointed	
	x̄	(N)	x̄	(N)	x̄	(N)
2-9 ACREAGE						
1960-61	40337.221	(113)	0.000	(6)	0.000	(1)
1964-65	41361.072	(111)	1427.143	(7)	0.000	(3)
1967-68	42522.125	(112)	0.000	(6)	0.000	(1)
1968-69	35013.208	(318)	18783.477	(130)	25491.887	(91)
1970-71	30476.152	(409)	16846.391	(151)	25594.089	(124)
2-10 REV. TOTAL (OPER)						
1960-61	235.844	(385)	69.151	(93)	370.969	(129)
1964-65	319.790	(438)	112.118	(127)	427.239	(163)
1967-68	368.683	(439)	128.301	(133)	669.567	(150)
1968-69	316.777	(341)	229.393	(122)	190.561	(98)
1960-71	291.993	(411)	108.806	(134)	132.163	(129)
2-11 REV. ASSESS LEVIES						
1960-61	46.602	(387)	24.344	(93)	236.102	(128)
1964-65	58.550	(438)	15.874	(127)	272.117	(163)
1967-68	67.732	(440)	31.263	(118)	378.320	(150)
1968-69	99.842	(341)	45.845	(110)	71.724	(98)
1970-71	98.697	(413)	46.555	(119)	72.256	(126)

Tables 2-9 through 2-13 (Cont.)

ACREAGE TOTAL REVENUE AND REVENUE FROM LEVY ASSESSMENT
AVERAGES BY METHOD OF SELECTION OF GOVERNING BODY

	POPULAR		PROPERTY QUALIFICATION		APPOINTED	
	$\bar{x}$	(N)	$\bar{x}$	(N)	$\bar{x}$	(N)
2-12 DEBT, TOTAL OUTS LONG TERM						
1960-61	1391.660	(385)	163.537	(67)	717.150	(127)
1964-65	1380.916	(440)	630.505	(105)	2567.920	(163)
1967-68	1513.448	(440)	1031.322	(115)	3449.265	(151)
1968-69	1165.235	(341)	881.255	(110)	1380.561	(98)
1970-71	1207.952	(413)	1185.875	(120)	1164.209	(129)
2-13 EXP. TOTAL (OPER.)						
1960-61	208.775	(386)	62.581	(93)	472.211	(128)
1964-65	281.899	(437)	98.039	(127)	387.472	(163)
1967-68	323.570	(435)	94.478	(134)	525.627	(150)
1968-69	291.487	(341)	91.285	(123)	140.010	(980)
1970-71	332.883	(410)	134.556	(135)	137.473	(129)

CONCLUSION

In this chapter, we have presented material which describes water districts in the state of California. As we have seen, there have been patterns of both growth and decline. In addition, we identified a pattern on which we will focus in the next section. Some of our variables indicated that there were clear differences between one person/one vote districts and property weighted districts and, in particular, that the former tended to exhibit much more stable behavior, while the latter were much more oscillatory in character. As we will see in the next chapter, this pattern holds when we examine other relationships. Having described some of the important dimensions of water districts in California, we turn to a consideration of a variety of relationships among our variables.

NOTES

1. Merrill R. Goodall, John D. Sullivan and Timothy De Young, "Statement" in U.S. Congress, Senate, Part 3 of Joint Hearings of the Interior and Insular Affairs Committee and the Small Business Committee on *Will the Family Farm Survive in America?* (Washington, D.C.: U.S. Government Printing Office, 1976).
2. In all tables in this chapter which contain data on revenues, expenditures, capital expenditures, and debts, that is to say, all tables which refer to money spent or received, the units are in thousands of dollars ($ 000).
3. All abbreviations for types of water districts which are in the tables in the next two chapters are described in Appendix E.

CHAPTER
3

Patterns of Financial Performance: Correlation Analysis and Proportions

Our analysis of the components of water districts' annual budgets yields comparable indices of fiscal allocation patterns. Special districts, like other public agencies, generate revenues, incur debt, and make expenditures. The majority of water districts generate revenue from two sources, tax levy assessment and service charges. We have developed measures from the California State Controller's budgetary data that indicate the relative allocation of capital resources as well as the proportional sources of revenue for each of our subgroupings. These measures may be useful in identifying the financing patterns of various types of water districts.

We are concerned initially with some basic patterns of financial performance. As we noted earlier, our interest here is focused in part on the districts grouped by the three types of methods of selecting the governing board: one person/one vote, property qualification, and county board appointed. We also have the data grouped by type of enabling act and, from time to time, we will present appropriate comparisons by enabling acts.

We present first an analysis of Controller data at the state and county level of aggregation for the years 1960–70. Reference is made to specific districts and areas to facilitate interpretation. We also present aggregate statistics for California Water Districts and other selected types of districts for the years 1960–74 in order to clarify and substantiate our data. Additionally, we expect to document the development of property qualification districts and to make some empirical statements about the economic viability of such districts.

CORRELATION ANALYSIS OF REVENUE, EXPENDITURE, INDEBTEDNESS, ACREAGE

A direct and understandable comparison is the correlation of revenue, indebtedness, expenditure, and acreage in the three categories of water districts where the method of selection of the governing board differs. In general, we anticipate a positive relationship among all of the four factors. For example, as the number of acres increases, the costs and revenues should proportionately increase. Indebtedness should correlate to a lesser extent with revenue, expenditure, and acreage since the total costs of a distribution system or participation in a federal or state project will usually be deferred over a long period of time. We do expect that the size of a district, either in terms of acreage or revenue base, should correlate to some extent with the amount of indebtedness.

There are a number of potentially confounding factors when we interpret the correlation of these variables. Acreage is especially relevant in agricultural and rural settings but probably is less influential than population density in urban settings. The correlation of revenue to expenditure traditionally has been used as an indicator of financial stability but legislative constraints on tax and service charges may affect this relationship. In general, we have assumed that the influence of these and other confounding factors is randomly distributed. In other words, intervening factors equally affect all types of sub-groups of water districts.

In this section we will depart from our previous mode of analysis and present some selected relationships among some variables in our data set. The mode of analysis, which we discussed above, will be the product-moment correlation coefficient. This coefficient can be considered to measure the strength of association between two variables. In addition, if one takes the correlation coefficient, typically labeled r, and squares it, the ensuing r^2 can be interpreted as the amount of total *variance* in one variable that can be attributed to another.

We present the relationship, for those years for which data are available, between total acreage and revenues, expenditures, and debt by type of political decision system. Blanks indicate that one or both variables are missing for that type of district for that year. In Table 3-1 the figures indicate differences among the three categories in reporting behavior and relative stability. Popularly elected districts are quite stable in the first three time periods, 1960-61, 1964-65, and 1967-68, and exhibit consistent reporting patterns. Property qualification districts and appointed districts by and large failed to report acreage figures until 1968-69. Appointed districts are extremely erratic in these later time periods, whereas property qualification districts show the strongest correlation with acreage. The decline in correlation for popular districts may be attributed to the change in format in 1968, where total revenues and expenditures were divided into operating and non-operating categories. Direct comparison of vertical trends is therefore not possible in this and the following tables; 1968-69 and 1970-71 should be considered separately from the first three time points, 1960-61, 1964-65, and 1967-68.

For one person/one vote districts, we can see that there is a strong relationship between total acreage and revenues and expenditures. This is not surprising as we would expect larger districts to have greater expenditures and to obtain in return higher revenues. The data for all years indicate that there is a rather poor relationship between acreage and debt. This suggests that large districts do not tend to incur larger amounts of debt than do smaller districts.

Turning to the year for which data are available for property qualification districts we observe a similar pattern with respect to expenditures and acreage, and the relationship is stronger than that observed for one person/one vote districts. Where there may be a negative relationship between acreage and revenue, we suggest that this can best be explained by noting that a disproportionately high number of the property qualification districts are "paper" organizations which have not started operations in a particular year. Thus they may have incurred expenses for legal and other start-up costs but have not yet begun to gain revenues. The same

Table 3-1

THE CORRELATION OF INDEBTEDNESS, REVENUE AND
EXPENDITURE WITH ACREAGE BY METHOD OF
SELECTION OF GOVERNING BODY

YEAR	POPULAR		PROPERTY QUALIFICATION		APPOINTED	
	$\bar{x}$	(N)	$\bar{x}$	(N)	$\bar{x}$	(N)
a. Indebtedness with Acreage						
1960-61	.58	(111)	-	(6)	-	(1)
1964-65	.54	(109)	.99	(7)	-	(3)
1967-68	.55	(109)	-	(6)	-	(1)
1968-69	.49	(314)	.55	(102)	.65	(91)
1970-71	.43	(405)	.59	(119)	.06 (124) [s=.253]	
b. Revenue with Acreage						
1960-61	.88	(111)	-	(6)	-	
1964-65	.87	(108)	.98	(7)	-	
1967-68	.87	(109)	-	(6)	-	
1968-69	.22	(313)	.63	(114)	.80	(91)
1970-71	.38	(402)	.76	(133)	.22	(124)
c. Expenditure with Acreage						
1960-61	.888	(111)	-	(6)	-	(1)
1964-65	.875	(108)	.99	(7)	-	(3)
1967-68	.90	(105)	-	(6)	-	(1)
1968-69	.50	(313)	.73	(115)	.80	(91)
1970-71	.36	(402)	.79	(134)	.22	(124)

s = Significance level. If no level is noted, then the probability of
s ≤ .05

explanation may hold for the relationships between acreage and debt.

The relevance of these correlation figures and the ones that follow are fairly clear. If the coefficients which appear seem both consistent and plausible, then we may assume that they are reliable and valid indicators of the relationships between various components of water district budgets. In the majority of cases, our data set yields reliable and valid correlation scores which demand interpretation where possible and which suggest various avenues worthy of additional analysis and research.

Table 3-1 in this sense exhibits fairly consistent correlations over time for two of our three types of districts: property qualification and one person/one vote districts. Appointed districts, on the other hand, exhibit correlations which vary radically when the number of appointed districts increases from 91 in 1968-69 to 124 in 1970-71. We must therefore conclude that either our data for these districts is untrustworthy in this case and/or hypothesize that the addition of new appointed districts produces random fluctuations in the correlation of acreage with indebtedness, revenue, and expenditure. If the latter is true, then new districts must be compared only to other new districts rather than to all districts of a certain type, since age seems to be a confounding factor in the correlation of budgetary components. Additional research could thus be directed toward the determination of the amount of time it takes a new district to become established and hence comparable to older districts.

Table 3-2 represents the relationships of revenue to expenditure in all categories. The correlation of indebtedness with revenue and expenditure (parts b and c of Table 3-2) seems to be increasing over time. Property qualification districts and appointed districts exhibit higher correlations between both indebtedness and expenditure and indebtedness and revenue. These higher correlations suggest relatively greater indebtedness among these districts. In one person/one vote districts, there is a very strong relationship between revenue and expenditures for all time points but a rather weaker relationship between revenue and debt. This suggests that this type of district gains revenue as a function of expenditures but does not tend to go into debt in order to generate revenue. In contrast, a high relationship between revenue and debt is observed for property qualification and appointed districts, which suggests that these districts tend to incur debt in order to generate revenue.

We have shown that one person/one vote districts tend to exhibit higher levels of public participation than do property qualification districts. Our findings also show that certain fiscal allocation patterns, such as the willingness to incur debt, are markedly different among our categories of water districts. One person/one vote districts, which tend to be more democratic in the selection of directors, also tend to generate revenue rather than incur indebtedness in order to cover expenditures. Democratic control, therefore, may promote relatively moderate fiscal policies. The willingness to incur indebtedness which is prevalent in property

Table 3-2

THE CORRELATION OF INDEBTEDNESS, REVENUE AND
EXPENDITURE BY METHOD OF SELECTION OF
GOVERNING BODY

YEAR	POPULAR		PROPERTY QUALIFICATION		APPOINTED	
	$\bar{x}$	(N)	$\bar{x}$	(N)	$\bar{x}$	(N)

a. Revenue with Expenditure

1960-61	.94	(385)	.99	(93)	.76	(128)
1964-65	.97	(437)	.69	(127)	.95	(163)
1967-68	.98	(435)	.94	(133)	.98	(150)
1968-69	.60	(341)	.72	(122)	.92	(98)
1970-71	.90	(410)	.97	(134)	.98	(129)

b. Indebtedness with Expenditure

1960-61	.33	(385)	.48	(67)	.51	(127)
1964-65	.49	(437)	.51	(105)	.96	(163)
1967-68	.56	(434)	.68	(114)	.93	(150)
1968-69	.56	(340)	.75	(110)	.87	(98)
1970-71	.31	(410)	.81	(120)	.80	(129)

c. Revenue with Indebtedness

1960-61	.35	(385)	.50	(67)	.08	(127)
1964-65	.49	(438)	.57	(105)	.96	(163)
1967-68	.54	(438)	.50	(114)	.95	(150)
1968-69	.24	(340)	.87	(110)	.72	(98)
1970-71	.31	(410)	84	(120)		

qualification and appointed districts may produce increased costs to the water consumer in the form of general and standby taxes. These tendencies are thus social policy decisions which can affect all members of the water community. In certain situations, one may suppose that grass roots opposition to increased taxes would provoke public protest. This is not possible in districts where the voter is, in effect, disenfranchised. In Berrenda Mesa Water District, for example, the passage of various bond issues has created an annual standby assessment of from $65.00 to over $75.00 per acre in addition to the general tax levy of $3.00 per acre. Our study of this district reveals that this tax schedule disproportionately burdens small farming enterprises. Small, individual landowners have steadily been replaced by larger, corporate enterprises which control the majority of votes and who can afford the tax burden.

Our analysis now turns to a comparison of district performance, which differs according to population density. Using the criteria and data of the *County and City Data Book, 1975* we divide the counties of California into three exclusive categories: urban, suburban, and rural. Appendix A lists the counties by category.

Table 3-3 examines the correlation of revenue and expenditure in different types of counties. The amount of variation accounted for in each category seems to be generally similar regardless of geographic setting. Suburban counties tend to show the strongest correlation figures. In this table and the following tables which examine water district performance in categories of counties with varying population density, we have employed the analysis of variance statistical technique. Simply stated, analysis of variance compares the amount of variation within a category to the amount of variation within each of the other categories and to the total variation of all categories. If, for example, the amount of variation in the correlation of revenue and expenditure in property qualification districts significantly varied between urban and suburban counties, analysis of variance techniques enables us to estimate the degree and importance of variation by comparison to established parameters of probability.

Table 3-4 presents a classification by regions of the relationship between indebtedness and acreage. The most prominent feature is of course the lack of data in property qualification and appointed districts in the first three time periods. There does seem to be a clear difference in performance among the three types of counties for the popularly elected districts. Acreage correlates better with indebtedness in suburban and rural settings for these types of districts.

Table 3-5 clearly shows a difference between property qualification and popular districts according to the degree of urbanization of the county. When we compare urban and suburban-rural districts we find that the correlation between revenue and expenditure differs significantly in such districts when the electoral system is one person/one vote. The correlation between revenue and acreage in property weighted districts in both urban and suburban-rural districts is similar. In property weighted districts the two correlations are .63 and .76; in popular districts the figures for the same years are quite dissimilar: .15 and .34 as compared to .95 and

Table 3-3

THE CORRELATION OF REVENUE WITH EXPENDITURE BY
METHOD OF SELECTION OF GOVERNING BODY
AND BY TYPE OF COUNTY

YEAR	POPULAR		PROPERTY QUALIFICATION		APPOINTED	
	$\bar{x}$	(N)	$\bar{x}$	(N)	$\bar{x}$	(N)
State Totals						
1960-61	.94	(385)	.99	(93)	.76	(128)
1964-65	.97	(437)	.69	(127)	.95	(163)
1967-68	.98	(435)	.94	(133)	.98	(150)
1968-69	.60	(341)	.72	(122)	.92	(98)
1970-71	.90	(410)	.97	(134)	.98	(129)
Urban Counties						
1960-61	.90	(258)	.99	(54)	.76	(110)
1964-65	.99	(277)	.71	(71)	.95	(129)
1967-68	.95	(274)	.94	(74)	.98	(122)
1968-69	.57	(223)	.75	(70)	.92	(86)
1970-71	.89	(250)	.97	(70)	.98	(112)
Suburban Counties						
1960-61	.99	(106)	.99	(38)	.98	(16)
1964-65	.99	(134)	.69	(51)	.99	(32)
1967-68	.99	(134)	.95	(53)	.99	(25)
1968-69	.94	(99)	.94	(45)	.96	(10)
1970-71	.94	(136)	.93	(56)	.99	(15)
Rural Counties						
1960-61	.99	(21)	–	(1)	–	(2)
1964-65	.32	(26)	.79	(5)	–	(2)
1967-68	.96	(27)	.96	(6)	–	(3)
1968-69	.99	(19)	.50	(7)	–	(2)
1970-71	.99	(24)	.85	(8)	–	(2)

Table 3-4

THE CORRELATION OF INDEBTEDNESS WITH ACREAGE BY
METHOD OF SELECTION OF GOVERNING BODY
AND BY TYPE OF COUNTY

YEAR	POPULAR		PROPERTY QUALIFICATION		APPOINTED	
	$\bar{x}$	(N)	$\bar{x}$	(N)	$\bar{x}$	(N)
State Totals						
1960-61	.58	(111)	–		–	
1964-65	.54	(109)	–		–	
1967-68	.55	(109)	–		–	
1968-69	.49	(314)	.55	(102)	.65	(91)
1970-71	.43	(405)	.59	(119)	.06	(124) [s=.4]
Urban Counties						
1960-61	.21	(57)	–		–	
1964-65	.23	(56)	–		–	
1967-68	.49	(56)	–		–	
1968-69	.62	(206)	.55	(54)	.65	(82)
1970-71	.66	(245)	.59	(58)	.07	(107) [s=.4]
Suburban Counties						
1960-61	.65	(46)	–		–	
1964-65	.56	(45)	–		–	
1967-68	.54	(45)	–		–	
1968-69	.79	(91)	.21	(41)	.99	(7)
1970-71	.45	(135)	.50	(53)	-.06	(15) [s=.416]
Rural Counties						
1960-61	.98	(8)	–		–	
1964-65	.96	(8)	–		–	
1967-68	.96	(8)	–		–	
1968-69	-.03	(17) [s=.461]	-.29	(7) [s=.27]	–	
1970-71	.22	(25) [s=.149]	-.25	(8) [s=.28]	–	

s = Significance level. If no level is noted, then the probability of $s \leq .05$.

Table 3-5

THE CORRELATION OF REVENUE WITH ACREAGE BY
METHOD OF SELECTION OF GOVERNING BODY
AND BY TYPE OF COUNTY

YEAR	POPULAR		PROPERTY QUALIFICATION		APPOINTED	
	$\bar{x}$	(N)	$\bar{x}$	(N)	$\bar{x}$	(N)
State Totals						
1960-61	.88	(111)	–		–	
1964-65	.87	(108)	.98	(7)	–	
1967-68	.87	(109)	–		–	
1968-69	.22	(313)	.63	(114)	.65	(91)
1970-71	.38	(402)	.76	(133)	.06	(124)[s=.253]
Urban Counties						
1960-61	.51	(57)	–		–	
1964-65	.53	(56)	.99	(5)	–	
1967-68	.52	(57)	–		–	
1968-69	.15	(206)	.63	(65)	.83	(82)
1970-71	.34	(245)	.76	(70)	.13	(107)
Suburban Counties						
1960-61	.97	(46)	–		–	
1964-65	.97	(44)	–		–	
1967-68	.98	(44)	–		–	
1968-69	.95	(91)	.73	(42)	.94	(7)
1970-71	.95	(133)	.66	(55)	.98	(15)
Rural Counties						
1960-61	.93	(8)	–		–	
1964-65	.93	(8)	–		–	
1967-68	.98	(8)	–		–	
1968-69	.18	(16)[s=.256]	-.32	(7)[s=.24]	–	
1970-71	.20	(24)[s=.18]	-.31	(8)[s=.23]	–	

s = Significance level. If no level is noted, then the probability of s = .05.

.95. We may therefore conclude that the fiscal management of property qualification districts tends to be extremely similar regardless of the population density of the county where it exists. Table 3-4 in retrospect may provide further substantiation for this conclusion.

One possible explanation for this finding is that property qualification districts tend to be agricultural in nature and therefore less responsive to variations in population density. If property qualification districts limited their services to irrigation, regardless of setting, we would expect little deviation in the correlation between acreage and revenue in urban and non-urban counties. Analysis of California Water Districts in Orange County, however, shows that irrigation sales account for little if any of the sales revenues these districts generate. A more plausible explanation, therefore, relates to the fact that residents in these districts are largely disenfranchised and therefore variations in population served does not affect decision making processes. Irvine Ranch Water District, for example, serves nearly 50,000 domestic users but has only 4 customers with voting powers. It should be added that the correlation of acreage with both revenue and expenditure in appointed districts exhibits radical fluctuations in both urban and suburban settings.

Tables 3-6, 3-7, and 3-8 follow the general patterns exhibited in Table 3-5 above. Popularly elected districts differ according to the type of county where they exist. Popular districts in suburban and rural counties consistently show higher correlation coefficients than in urban areas. Table 3-6, for example, dramatically shows that acreage is an extremely strong indicator of expenditure level in suburban counties but is not nearly as strong in urban settings. Property qualification districts contrast sharply from these patterns, as indicated by the similar correlations in urban and suburban counties.

Our correlational material presented above thus indicates that both the method of selection of governing body and the type of county where the district exists influence the correlation of budgetary and size components of a water district. Revenue tends to correlate quite well with expenditure and acreage and to a lesser extent with indebtedness. Acreage becomes less important as one moves to an urban setting, except for property qualification districts. These districts tend to perform similarly regardless of variation in population density.

Table 3-6

THE CORRELATION OF EXPENDITURE WITH ACREAGE
METHOD OF SELECTION OF GOVERNING BODY
AND BY TYPE OF COUNTY

YEAR	POPULAR		PROPERTY QUALIFICATION		APPOINTED	
	$\bar{x}$	(N)	$\bar{x}$	(N)	$\bar{x}$	(N)
State Totals						
1960-61	.89	(111)	-	(6)	-	(1)
1964-65	.88	(108)	.99	(7)	-	
1967-68	.90	(105)	-	(6)	-	(1)
1968-69	.50	(313)	.73	(115)	.80	(91)
1970-71	.36	(402)	.79	(134)	.22	(124)
Urban Counties						
1960-61	.56	(57)	-	(4)	-	
1964-65	.55	(56)	.99	(5)	-	
1967-68	.55	(53)	-	(4)	-	
1968-69	.49	(206)	.72	(65)	.80	(82)
1970-71	.38	(245)	.78	(70)	.20	(107)
Suburban Counties						
1960-61	.98	(46)	-	(2)	-	
1964-65	.98	(44)	-	(2)	-	(22)
1967-68	.98	(44)	-	(2)	-	
1968-69	.96	(91)	.78	(43)	.99	(7)
1970-71	.96	(133)	.73	(56)	.96	(15)
Rural Counties						
1960-61	.95	(8)	-		-	
1964-65	.99	(8)	-		-	
1967-68	.99	(8)	-		-	
1968-69	.19	(16) [s=.243]	-.35	(7) [s=.22]	-	(2)
1970-71	.25	(26) [s=.12]	-.29	(8) [s=.25]		

$p < .05$

Table 3-7

THE CORRELATION OF REVENUE WITH INDEBTEDNESS
METHOD OF SELECTION OF GOVERNING BODY
AND BY TYPE OF COUNTY

YEAR	POPULAR		PROPERTY QUALIFICATION		APPOINTED	
	$\bar{x}$	(N)	$\bar{x}$	(N)	$\bar{x}$	(N)
State Totals						
1960-61	.35	(385)	.50	(67)	.08	(127)
1964-65	.49	(438)	.57	(105)	.96	(163)
1967-68	.54	(438)	.50	(114)	.95	(150)
1968-69	.24	(340)	.87	(110)	.72	(98)
1970-71	.31	(410)	.84	(120)	.76	(129)
Urban Counties						
1960-61	.08	(258)	.33	(33)	.07	(109)
1964-65	.48	(278)	.49	(52)	.96	(129)
1967-68	.66	(277)	.52	(57)	.95	(122)
1968-69	.18	(223)	.89	(59)	.71	(86)
1970-71	.31	(250)	.86	(58)	.76	(112)
Suburban Counties						
1960-61	.69	(106)	.65	(33)	-.10	(16)
1964-65	.62	(134)	.81	(48)	.96	(32)
1967-68	.57	(134)	.35	(51)	.97	(25)
1968-69	.78	(98)	.07	(44)	.90	(10)
1970-71	.36	(136)	.25	(54)	.13	(15)
Rural Counties						
1960-61	.98	(21)	-		-	
1964-65	.79	(26)	.97	(5)	-	
1967-68	.85	(27)	.70	(6)	-	
1968-69	.36	(19)	.41	(7)	-	
1970-71	.72	(24)	.79	(8)	-	

$p < .05$

Table 3-8

THE CORRELATION OF EXPENDITURE WITH INDEBTEDNESS, METHOD
OF SELECTION OF GOVERNING BODY AND
BY TYPE OF COUNTY

YEAR	POPULAR		PROPERTY QUALIFICATION		APPOINTED	
	$\bar{x}$	(N)	$\bar{x}$	(N)	$\bar{x}$	(N)
State Totals						
1960-61	.33	(385)	.48	(67)	.51	(127)
1964-65	.49	(437)	.51	(105)	.96	(163)
1967-68	.56	(434)	.68	(114)	.93	(150)
1968-69	.56	(340)	.75	(110)	.87	(98)
1970-71	.31	(410)	.81	(120)	.80	(129)
Urban Counties						
1960-61	.11	(258)	.33	(33)	.51	(109)
1964-65	.42	(277)	.52	(52)	.96	(129)
1967-68	.66	(273)	.74	(57)	.94	(122)
1968-69	.49	(223)	.79	(59)	.87	(86)
1970-71	.28	(250)	.82	(58)	.80	(112)
Suburban Counties						
1960-61	.69	(106)	.65	(33)	-.19	(16)
1964-65	.65	(134)	.35	(48)	.97	(32)
1967-68	.58	(134)	.34	(51)	.95	(25)
1968-69	.05	(98)	.27	(44)	.95	(10)
1970-71	.53	(136)	.53	(54)	.20	(15)
Rural Counties						
1960-61	.97	(21)	-		-	
1964-65	.24	(26)	.79	(5)	-	
1967-68	.96	(27)	.83	(6)	-	
1968-69	.32	(19)	.99	(7)	-	
1970-71	.72	(24)	.36	(8)	-	

$p < .05$

COMPUTED INDICATORS

The proportions which follow were computed from the Controller data. Variables and formulae used are listed in Appendix C. Each of the proportions can be directly interpreted as percentages. Once again, there will be some variation in the figures after 1968 because of the change in format of the Controller data. Computed variables are compared according to type of district, method of selection of governing board, and type of county. We may regard these averages as indicators of the most commonly occurring fiscal allocation proportions. We expect variations according to the type of district, the geographical location of the district, and the demographic characteristics of the district. In addition, we are specifically concerned with variations caused by differences in the method of selection of the governing body, since the funding and expenditure policies in water districts relate directly to measures of equity and efficiency in the management of water resources.

REVENUE MEASURES

Using the aggregated revenue proportions reported by all districts in the years 1968-69 and 1970-71, we may compare the various subsets of districts and types to state averages. For example, the major sources from which operating revenues were derived in 1968-69 are as follows, according to the State Controller's reports:

Source	*Percent of Total*
Water sales	
Residential	24.8
Business	1.8
Industrial	2.5
Irrigation	17.7
Sales for Resale	42.0
Interdepartmental	.6
All Others	2.2
Water Services	
Fire Prevention	.3
Ground Water Replenishment	2.3

68 *California Water: A New Political Economy*

In sum, the state averages for irrigation sales are 17.7 percent and those for domestic sales are 29.2 percent. We now present a descriptive summary of the revenue measures, suggested by categories of revenue that appear in the Controller reports.

Net Income-Loss Revenue Proportion of Total Revenues

This variable is the quotient of net income or loss divided by total revenues. One might expect that a public agency would strive for a balanced budget, but variations are expected for districts that anticipate revenues and/or expenditures at some later point in time (e.g., a new district that anticipates increased water service revenues after the completion of a distribution system may accrue a net loss until the system is functioning). The smaller the figure that appears, the closer the district is to a balanced budget (Table 3-9).

Sales and/or Service Charges as a Proportion of Total Revenues

We compare both the total sales and service charge proportions of total revenues and also look at the proportions of different types of sales in the following categories: a) irrigation sales, b) domestic sales —a combination of residential, business, and industrial sales (Tables 3-10, 3-11, and 3-12).

Levy Revenues Proportion of Total Revenues

It is important to compare this proportion to the preceding indicator, the sales revenue proportion, since these variables represent the two primary sources of revenue for the majority of water districts in California. Additionally, this indicator seems to correlate positively with the amount of indebtedness, since levies are generally assessed to repay bond commitments. It should also be noted that the basis for levy assessment differs in different types of districts. Property qualification districts assess land only, whereas the majority of popular and appointed districts assess all property. Irrigation districts are one of the few popular districts which similarly assess land only.

Table 3-9

NET OPERATING INCOME - OR LOSS - AS A PROPORTION OF
TOTAL REVENUES BY TYPE OF DISTRICT AND BY
METHOD OF SELECTION OF GOVERNING BODY[1]

	P60 $\bar{x}$ (N) s.d.[a]	P64 $\bar{x}$ (N) s.d.	P67 $\bar{x}$ (N) s.d.	P68 $\bar{x}$ (N) s.d.	P70 $\bar{x}$ (N) s.d.
IRR	.08 (99) .28	.05 (99) .28	.09 (94) .29	-.10 (58) .32	-.21 (62) .37
CSA	.05 (2) .07	.15 (2) .29	.39 (4) .39	.16 (2) .25	-.09 (4) .66
MTR	-.01 (1) .-	.44 (1) -	.35 (1) -	.94 (1) -	.43 (1) -
CAL	.19 (60) .33	.17 (75) .36	.19 (84) .30	-.02 (54) .39	-.08 (58) .30
MIM	.34 (1) -	.79 (1) -	.53 (2) .16	-	.19 (3) .41
CMS	.28 (62) .40	.26 (88) .41	.24 (100) .38	.15 (8) .40	-.01 (49) .40
CWT	.27 (124) .44	.18 (136) .37	.20 (139) .36	.03 (119) .34	-.04 (127) .33
FCN	.18 (27) .35	.21 (26) .34	.10 (26) .30	.50 (2) .17	.34 (5) .41
MNT	.10 (10) .40	.20 (26) .52	-.02 (26) .65	-	-.26 (3) .65
HPT	.20 (1) .-	.71 (1) -	.32 (1) -	.43 (1) -	.86 (1) -
RCP	-	.44 (6) .15	.28 (18) .46	-	.03 (3) .58
RCM	.19 (1) -	.07 (1) -	.07 (1) -	-	.50 (1) -
MUT	.21 (3) .15	-.13 (3) .13	-.13 (3) .21	.37 (1) -	-.64 (2) .51
PUT	.19 (36) .35	.18 (36) .35	.16 (37) .30	-.02 (8) .36	-.05 (34) .35
REP	-	-	-	-	-
STR	.23 (6) .37	.50 (6) .14	.29 (6) .28	.43 (1) -	.14 (6) .37
CNV	.12 (8) .38	.33 (8) .28	.17 (11) .42	.24 (4) .15	-.04 (8) .44
MWT	.21 (38) .50	.23 (40) .29	.18 (35) .35	-.09 (26) .26	-.08 (28) .30
CWK	.11 (74) .36	.20 (82) .38	.13 (79) .34	-.11 (69) .38	-.06 (68) .37
WAG	.19 (15) .34	.19 (15) .36	.34 (15) .33	.23 (12) .31	.10 (10) .24
POPULAR	.21 (328) .40	.17 (374) .36	.18 (393) .36	-.01 (214) .33	-.08 (275) .37
PROPERTY QUALIFICATION	.19 (75) .33	.20 (90) .35	.19 (102) .31	.01 (59) .39	-.06 (73) .33
APPOINTED	.12 (112) .36	.20 (135) .40	.10 (132) .41	-.09 (72) .39	-.03 (77) .40

a s.d. indicates the standard deviation.

Table 3-10

SALES REVENUE PROPORTION OF TOTAL REVENUES
BY METHOD OF SELECTION AND BY
TYPE OF COUNTY[2]

YEAR	POPULAR			PROPERTY QUALIFICATION			APPOINTED		
	$\bar{x}$	(N)	s.d.	$\bar{x}$	(N)	s.d.	$\bar{x}$	(N)	s.d.
State Totals									
1960-61	.48	(338)	.40*	.59	(66)	.41	.52	(115)	.44
1964-65	.49	(372)	.38*	.59	(90)	.41	.46	(139)	.45
1967-68	.51	(392)	.37*	.55	(102)	.40	.50	(138)	.42
1968-69	.40	(202)	.32*	.34	(76)	.38	.40	(90)	.30
1970-71	.42	(360)	.31	.43	(83)	.39	.33	(121)	.31
Urban Counties									
1960-61	.50	(237)	.40	.60	(40)	.45	.56	(99)	.44
1964-65	.52	(249)	.37	.62	(48)	.43	.49	(17)	.45
1967-68	.53	(249)	.36	.54	(58)	.42	.53	(15)	.42
1968-69	.42	(205)	.32	.27	(45)	.36	.39	(80)	.29
1970-71	.42	(231)	.31	.37	(41)	.37	.31	(106)	.30
Suburban Counties									
1960-61	.47	(83)	.38	.56	(25)	.34	.30	(14)	.40
1964-65	.50	(99)	.37	.59	(39)	.38	.30	(20)	.40
1967-68	.52	(116)	.37	.59	(41)	.36	.39	(20)	.42
1968-69	.41	(79)	.31	.46	(28)	.41	.49	(8)	.36
1970-71	.43	(109)	.32	.50	(39)	.40	.52	(13)	.37
Rural Counties									
1960-61	.26	(18)	.33	1.0	(1)	—	.50	(2)	.71
1964-65	.19	(24)	.30	.29	(3)	.26	.50	(2)	.71
1967-68	.23	(27)	.35	.22	(3)	.38	.32	(3)	.56
1968-69	.23	(18)	.26	.31	(3)	.27	.41	(2)	.59
1970-71	.26	(20)	.26	.32	(3)	.28	.38	(2)	.53

* = $p < .05$

Table 3-11

SALES REVENUE PROPORTION OF TOTAL
REVENUES BY TYPE OF DISTRICT

	S60 x̄ (N) s.d.	S64 x̄ (N) s.d.	S67 x̄ (N) s.d.	S68 x̄ (N) s.d.	S70 x̄ (N) s.d.
IRR	.51(100).35	.55 (96).33	.54 (96).32	.39 (94).30	.38 (94).29
CSA	–	–	.11 (04).12	–	.50 (04).35
MTR	–	–	–	–	–
CAL	.62 (50).43	.63 (73).42	.56 (84).41	.34 (67).39	.39 (66).39
MIM	–	–	–	–	–
CMS	.36 (63).41	.36 (85).40	.39 (97).39	.30 (08).23	.51 (52).29
CWT	.58(129).39	.59(139).36	.63(138).33	.41(160).32	.43(162).31
FCN	.03 (28).06	.04 (27).07	.09 (28).20	. –	.51 (07).44
MNT	–	.05 (26).20	.16 (27).33	–	.01 (24).01
HPT	–	–	–	–	–
RCP	–	.02 (07).03	.08 (18).24	–	–
RCM	–	–	–	–	–
MUT	–	–	–	–	–
PUT	.62 (34).25	.54 (37).28	.53 (36).30	.58 (10).28	.51 (39).33
REP	–	–	–	–	–
STR	.73 (06).25	.59 (06).22	.50 (06).29	–	.69 (06).25
CNV	.34 (09).31	.34 (10).34	.52 (11).35	.30 (08).37	.52 (10).39
MWT	.31 (42).39	.43 (41).39	.54 (37).37	.39 (37).36	.35 (76).33
CWK	.77 (76).33	.73 (85).38	.76 (82).30	.39 (86).28	.41 (89).28
WAG	.50 (15).44	.58 (15).45	.29 (16).46	.45 (16).34	.41 (15).37
POPULAR	.48(338).40	.49(372).38	.58(392).37	.40(302).32	.42(360).31
PROPERTY QUALIFI- CATION	.59 (66).41	.59 (90).41	.55(102).40	.34 (76).38	.43 (83).39
APPOINTED	.52(115).44	.46(139).45	.50(138).42	.40 (90).30	.33(121).31

Table 3-12

DOMESTIC AND IRRIGATION SALES REVENUE PROPORTION OF
TOTAL SALES REVENUES FOR 1968 and 1970
BY TYPE OF DISTRICT

	Domestic 68 $\bar{x}$ (N) s.d.	Domestic 70 $\bar{x}$ (N) s.d.	Irrigation 68 $\bar{x}$ (N) s.d.	Irrigation 70 $\bar{x}$ (N) s.d.
IRR	.08 (97) .14	.08 (97) .14	.17 (97) .16	.16 (97) .16
CSA	.45 (2) .08	.31 (4) .14	0 (4) -	0 (4) -
MTR	-	-	-	-
CAL	.05 (70) .12	.07 (69) .13	.16 (76) .20	.17 (76) .21
MIM	-	.05 (2) .07	-	-
CMS	.24 (10) .16	.34 (58) .18	.01 (10) .01	.01 (58) .03
CWT	.24 (161) .17	.25 (163) .17	.02 (161) .06	.02 (163) .07
FCN	0 (3) -	.07 (7) .19	.17 (3) .28	.14 (7) .23
MNT	-	.01 (24) .01	-	0 (24) -
HPT	.50 (1) -	0 (1) -	0 (1) -	0 (1) -
RCP	-	.17 (8) .21	-	0 (8) -
RCM	-	0 (1) -	-	.44 (1) -
MUT	0 (1) -	.01 (3) .01	.50 (1) -	.24 (3) .22
PUT	.31 (10) .18	.30 (42) .17	.04 (10) .10	.02 (42) .07
REP	-	-	-	-
STR	.33 (1) -	.40 (6) .10	-	-
CNV	.13 (8) .18	.21 (10) .23	.06 (8) .15	.08 (10) .18
MWT	.10 (38) .15	.09 (39) .13	.04 (38) .07	.05 (39) .09
CWK	.25 (87) .16	.25 (89) .16	.01 (87) .03	.01 (89) .04
WAG	.23 (16) .19	.20 (15) .20	.04 (16) .07	.02 (15) .06
POPULAR	.30 (307) .31	.30 (368) .30	.08 (309) .16	.06 (368) .14
PROPERTY QUALIFI-CATION	.06 (80) .13	.10 (87) .16	.15 (86) .20	.15 (94) .20
APPOINTED	.25 (91) .17	.19 (123) .18	.01 (91) .06	.01 (123) .06

Finally, a relatively high levy revenue proportion "equally" distributes the financial burden of water service without regard to differential water consumption. Our study of Berrenda Mesa Water District, a property qualification district, reveals that the standby levy, a tax assessed to all landowners whether they have consumed water or not, acts as a mechanism of exclusion for those unable to withstand the financial burden (Tables 3-13 and 3-14).

EXPENDITURE MEASURES

Administrative Expenditure as a Proportion of Total Expenditures

This indicator offers a number of valuable interpretations. The administrative overhead figure can be considered an indicator of performance efficiency if variations in non-administrative expenditures vary randomly for all districts. We may expect, though, that newer districts would exhibit relatively lower scores, since other expenditures would tend to be quite large (e.g., the construction of a distribution system). Additionally, selection of those districts where the administrative proportion exceeds a certain value will enable us to determine the identity and relative frequency of "paper districts."

Depreciation and Amortization Expenditures as a Proportion of Total Expenditure

In general this proportion is an indicator of the age of a district as well as the bonded indebtedness. A high proportion may indicate a willingness and/or ability to allocate capital for depreciation expenses (Table 3-15).

Utility Plant Depletion Additions Proportion of Total Expenditure

This variable is, in general, an indicator of age of a district's utility plant and its propensity to allocate capital (Table 3-15).

Table 3-13

LEVY REVENUE PROPORTION OF TOTAL REVENUES BY
METHOD OF SELECTION OF GOVERNING
BODY AND BY TYPE OF COUNTY

Year	Popular			Property Qualification			Appointed		
	x̄	(N)	s.d.	x̄	(N)	s.d.	x̄	(N)	s.d.
State Totals									
1960-61	.38	(289)	.39*	.31	(75)	.38	.35	(111)	.40
1964-65	.38	(325)	.37*	.28	(93)	.36*	.41	(133)	.43
1967-68	.34	(391)	.35*	.40	(90)	.37	.38	(142)	.41
1968-69	.23	(312)	.21	.20	(80)	.18	.21	(92)	.16
1970-71	.24	(308)	.22	.23	(87)	.20	.20	(94)	.17
Urban Counties									
1960-61	.35	(229)	.38	.29	(44)	.41	.34	(98)	.41
1964-65	.35	(245)	.36	.21	(49)	.34	.41	(113)	.43
1967-68	.35	(250)	.34	.39	(48)	.39	.34	(116)	.39
1968-69	.19	(208)	.14	.20	(50)	.20	.21	(81)	.16
1970-71	.02	(204)	.16	.23	(47)	.16	.20	(83)	.16
Suburban Counties									
1960-61	.35	(85)	.39	.32	(29)	.33	.53	(13)	.38
1964-65	.39	(108)	.36	.31	(40)	.25	.50	(20)	.42
1967-68	.38	(125)	.35	.35	(38)	.32	.56	(21)	.41
1968-69	.22	(87)	.19	.20	(34)	.15	.21	(9)	.18
1970-71	.20	(88)	.16	.21	(36)	.23	.19	(9)	.16
Rural Counties									
1960-61	.35	(17)	.39	0	(0)	0	.50	(2)	.71
1964-65	.65	(22)	.39	.70	(3)	.26	0	(1)	0
1967-68	.57	(27)	.41	.77	(3)	.38	.3	(3)	.58
1968-69	.24	(19)	.14	.15	(3)	.10	.20	(2)	.19
1970-71	.25	(19)	.15	.28	(3)	.09	.30	(2)	.29

* = ≤ .05

Table 3-14

LEVY REVENUE PROPORTION OF TOTAL REVENUES
BY TYPE OF DISTRICT

	L60 x̄ (N) s.d.	L64 x̄ (N) s.d.	L67 x̄ (N) s.d.	L68 x̄ (N) s.d.	L70 x̄ (N) s.d.
IRR	.37 (99) .35	.30 (97) .30	.34 (99) .31	.18 (99) .13	.17 (99) .12
CSA	-	.83 (2) .24	.59 (4) .41	.06 (2) .08	.10 (2) .14
MTR	.33 (1) .-	.21 (1) -	.37 (1) -	.43 (1) -	.45 (1) -
CAL	.26 (59) .39	.24 (75) .36	.39 (71) .38	.20 (78) .19	.23 (77) .20
MIM	.45 (2) .30	.21 (2) .30	.71 (2) .40	-	-
CMS	.46 (61) .42	.53 (87) .40	.51 (100) .38	.19 (11) .17	.17 (11) .16
CWT	.32 (130) .38	.29 (138) .35	.28 (140) .32	.22 (162) .17	.23 (159) .18
FCN	.74 (26) .28	.61 (26) .35	.60 (28) .32	.39 (3) .54	.41 (3) .53
MNT	1.0 (10) .0	.94 (24) .21	.80 (28) .36	-	-
HPT	.58 (1) -	.62 (1) -	.58 (1) -	0 (1) -	0 (1) -
RCP	-	.96 (7) .06	.62 (18) .45	-	-
RCM	0 (1) -	0 (1) -	.01 (1) -	-	-
MUT	-	-	-	-	-
PUT	.33 (36) .26	.35 (39) .29	.32 (38) .27	.15 (10.12	.15 (11) .10
REP	-	-	-	-	-
STR	.27 (06) .25	.38 (6) .22	.45 (6) .32	.27 (1) -	.27 (1) -
CNV	.59 (8) .32	.47 (10) .37	.35 (11) .33	.24 (8) .15	.14 (8) .13
MWT	.47 (36) .43	.38 (41) .35	.30 (38) .30	.18 (39) .15	.22 (39) .15
CWK	.16 (76) .28	.21 (83) .35	.16 (83) .27	.21 (88) .14	.20 (90) .14
WAG	.43 (15) .44	.21 (14) .37	.32 (16) .43	.17 (16) .19	.11 (14) .16
POPULAR	.38 (289) .39	.38 (325) .37	.34 (391) .35	.23 (312) .21	.24 (308) .22
PROPERTY QUALIFI- CATION	.31 (75) .38	.28 (93) .36	.40 (93) .36	.20 (80) .18	.23 (87) .20
APPOINTED	.35 (111) .40	.41 (133) .43	.38 (142) .41	.21 (92) .16	.20 (94) .17

Table 3-15

Table 3-15 a: Depreciation, Amortization Expenditure Proportion of Total Operating Expenditures of Type of District
b: Utility Depletion Additions Expenditure Proportion of Total Expenditure by Type of District

	a. DA68 x̄ (N) s.d.	DA70 x̄ (N) s.d.	b. U68 x̄ (N) s.d.	U70 x̄ (N) s.d.
IRR	.10 (98) .10	.12 (97) .10	.14 (98) .18	.15 (97) .19
CSA	0 (2) -	.10 (4) .20	0 (2) -	.16 (4) .23
MTR	.74 (1) -	.21 (1) -	.98 (1) -	.83 (1) -
CAL	.06 (66) .11	.10 (73) .13	.17 (68) .28	.14 (74) .27
MIM	. -	.02 (3) .05	-	.15 (3) .14
CMS	.08 (11) .12	.15 (57) .12	.32 (11) .33	.19 (57) .23
CWT	.14 (146) .11	.16 (153) .10	.28 (146) .28	.25 (153) .23
FCN	.10 (3) .28	.04 (5) .05	.24 (2) .08	.22 (6) .39
MNT	-	0 (24) -	-	.02 (24) .08
HPT	0 (1) -	0 (1) -	0 (1) -	0 (1) -
RCP	-	.09 (8) .14	-	.09 (8) .09
RCM	-	0 (1) -	-	0 (1) -
MUT	0 (1) -	0 (3) -	0 (1) -	.02 (3) .03
PUT	.14 (10) .09	.17 (41) .15	.24 (10) .34	.21 (41) .27
REP	-	-	-	-
STR	.22 (1) -	.19 (6) .06	0 (1) -	.23 (6) .25
CNV	.02 (8) .07	.15 (10) .20	.09 (8) .12	.20 (10) .21
MWT	.07 (39) .10	.08 (38) .09	.19 (39) .27	.26 (38) .31
CWK	.15 (84) .10	.16 (84) .12	.15 (85) .24	.19 (85) .26
WAG	.02 (14) .04	.08 (14) .08	.38 (15) .41	.23 (14) .34
POPULAR	.13 (288) .14	.13 (353) .12	.31 (290) .31	.27 (361) .28
PROPERTY QUALIFICATION	.06 (76) .11	.10 (92) .14	.17 (78) .28	.17 (93) .27
APPOINTED	.14 (87) .11	.12 (116) .12	.15 (88) .24	.15 (118) .25

Table 3-16 combines the profit-loss comparisons of different types of districts with the three categories of districts as determined by differences in the method of selection of the governing board. Beginning with the bottom three rows of the table, we can see that appointed districts seem to generate less profit than either popular or property qualification districts. That is to say that the budgets in this category tend to be more nearly balanced than in the other two categories. Once again we note the incomparability of 1968-71 figures to the earlier time periods. Community Service Districts and County Water Districts are two types of districts which tend to generate as much as 50 percent excess profit whereas Irrigation Districts, similar in function but different in terms of the method of selection of the governing board, exhibit the lowest profit proportions. Although no analysis has yet been done which considers urban and rural variations, our case studies of California Water Districts in Orange County reveal that there may be wide variations in net profit in urban areas.

Table 3-17 represents the first example of our analysis of variance technique which statistically determines whether there is a significant difference in performance between urban, rural, and suburban counties. The asterisks clearly show the continuation of a trend noted in Tables 3-4 and 3-5 above. Popular districts in this case exhibit significantly different levy to revenue proportions in rural counties where the proportion is much smaller than in urban or suburban counties. Table 3-10 shows a remarkable degree of consistency between the types of districts and the levy proportion over time. In the first three time periods, 1960-61, 1964-65, and 1967-68, all districts received from 28 percent to 41 percent of their revenue from levy assessments. In the last two time periods, 1968-69 and 1970-71, an even greater degree of homogeneity is apparent since the levy proportion of revenues varies only from 20 to 24 percent. The separation of operating revenues from non-operating revenues accounts for the decline in magnitude and also suggests that variations in non-operating revenues are more common than variations in sources of operating revenues. In general, these proportions can best be utilized as standards of typical performance by which we can evaluate individual districts.

Table 3-16

NET OPERATING INCOME - OR LOSS - AS A PROPORTION
OF TOTAL REVENUES BY TYPE OF DISTRICT AND
BY METHOD OF SELECTION OF GOVERNING BODY

	P60 $\bar{x}$ (N) s.d.	P64 $\bar{x}$ (N) s.d.	P67 $\bar{x}$ (N) s.d.	P68 $\bar{x}$ (N) s.d.	P70 $\bar{x}$ (N) s.d.
IRR	.08 (99) .28	.05 (99) .28	.09 (94) .29	-.10 (58) .32	-.21 (62) .37
CSA	.05 (2) .07	.15 (2) .29	.39 (4) .39	.16 (2) .25	-.09 (4) .66
MTR	.01 (1) -	.44 (1) -	.35 (1) -	.94 (1) -	.43 (1) -
CAL	.19 (60) .33	.17 (75) .36	.19 (84) .30	-.02 (54) .39	-.08 (58) .30
MIM	.34 (1) -	.79 (1) -	.53 (2) .16	-	.19 (3) .41
CMS	.28 (62) .40	.26 (88) .41	.24 (100) .38	.15 (8) .40	-.01 (49) .40
CWT	.27 (124) .44	.18 (136) .17	.20 (139) .36	.03 (119) .34	-.04 (127) .33
FCN	.18 (27) .35	.21 (26) .34	.10 (26) .30	.50 (2) .17	.34 (5) .41
MNT	.10 (10) .40	.20 (26) .52	-.02 (26) .65	-	-.26 (3) .65
HPT	.20 (1) -	.71 (1) -	.32 (1) -	.43 (1) -	.86 (1) -
RCP	-	.44 (6) .15	.28 (18) .46	-	.03 (3) .58
RCM	.19 (1) -	.07 (1) -	.07 (1) -	-	-.50 (1) -
MUT	.21 (3) .15	-.13 (3) .13	-.13 (3) .21	.37 (1) -	-.64 (2) .51
PUT	.19 (36) .35	.18 (36) .35	.16 (37) .30	-.02 (8) .36	-.05 (34) .35
REP	-	-	-	-	-
STR	.23 (6) .37	.50 (6) .14	.29 (6) .28	.43 (1) -	.14 (6) .37
CNV	.12 (8) .38	.33 (8) .28	.17 (11) .42	.25 (4) .15	-.04 (8) .44
MWT	.21 (38) .50	.23 (40) .29	.18 (35) .35	-.09 (26) .26	-.08 (28) .30
CWK	.11 (74) .36	.20 (82) .38	.13 (79) .34	-.11 (69) .38	-.06 (68) .37
WAG	.19 (15) .34	.19 (15) .36	.34 (15) .33	.23 (12) .31	.10 (10) .24
POPULAR	.21 (328) .40	.17 (374) .36	.18 (393) .36	-.01 (214) .33	-.08 (275) .37
PROPERTY QUALIFI-CATION	.19 (75) .33	.20 (90) .35	.19 (102) .31	.01 (59) .39	-.06 (73) .33
APPOINTED	.12 (112) .36	.20 (135) .40	.10 (132) .41	-.09 (72) .39	-.03 (77) .40

Table 3-17

LEVY REVENUE PROPORTION OF TOTAL REVENUES
BY METHOD OF SELECTION OF GOVERNING
BODY AND BY TYPE OF COUNTY

YEAR	POPULAR			PROPERTY QUALIFICATION			APPOINTED		
	$\bar{x}$	(N)	s.d.	$\bar{x}$	(N)	s.d.	$\bar{x}$	(N)	s.d.
State Totals									
1960-61	.38	(289)	.39*	.31	(75)	.38	.35	(111)	.40
1964-65	.38	(325)	.37*	.28	(93)	.36*	.41	(133)	.43
1967-68	.34	(391)	.35*	.40	(90)	.37	.38	(142)	.41
1968-69	.23	(312)	.21	.20	(80)	.18	.21	(92)	.16
1970-71	.24	(308)	.22	.23	(87)	.20	.20	(94)	.17
Urban Counties									
1960-61	.35	(229)	.38	.29	(44)	.41	.34	(98)	.41
1964-65	.35	(245)	.36	.21	(49)	.34	.41	(113)	.43
1967-68	.35	(250)	.34	.39	(48)	.39	.34	(116)	.39
1968-69	.19	(208)	.14	.20	(50)	.20	.21	(81)	.16
1970-71	.20	(204)	.16	.23	(47)	.16	.20	(83)	.16
Suburban Counties									
1960-61	.35	(85)	.39	.32	(29)	.33	.53	(13)	.38
1964-65	.39	(108)	.36	.31	(40)	.25	.50	(20)	.42
1967-68	.38	(125)	.35	.35	(38)	.32	.56	(21)	.41
1968-69	.22	(87)	.19	.20	(34)	.15	.21	(9)	.18
1970-71	.20	(88)	.16	.21	(36)	.23	.19	(9)	.16
Rural Counties									
1960-61	.35	(17)	.39	0	(0)	0	.50	(2)	.71
1964-65	.65	(22)	.39	.70	(3)	.26	0	(1)	0
1967-68	.57	(27)	.41	.77	(3)	.38	.3	(3)	.58
1968-69	.24	(19)	.14	.15	(3)	.10	.20	(2)	.19
1970-71	.25	(19)	.15	.28	(3)	.09	.30	(2)	.29

* = $<$ .05

Table 3-18

LEVY REVENUE PROPORTION OF TOTAL REVENUES
BY TYPE OF DISTRICT

	L60 x̄ (N) s.d.	L64 x̄ (N) s.d.	L67 x̄ (N) s.d.	L68 x̄ (N) s.d.	L70 x̄ (N) s.d.
IRR	.37 (99) .35	.30 (97) .30	.34 (99) .31	.18 (99) .13	.17 (99) .12
CSA	-	.83 (2) .24	.59 (4) .14	.06 (2) .08	.10 (2) .14
MTR	.33 (1) -	.21 (1) -	.37 (1) -	.43 (1) -	.45 (1) -
CAL	.26 (59) .39	.24 (75) .36	.39 (71) .38	.20 (78) .19	.23 (77) .20
MIM	.45 (2) .30	.21 (2) .30	.71 (2) .40	-	-
CMS	.46 (61) .42	.53 (87) .40	.51 (100) .38	.19 (11) .17	.17 (11) .16
CWT	.32 (130) .38	.29 (138) .35	.28 (140) .32	.22 (162) .17	.23 (159) .18
FCN	.74 (26) .28	.61 (26) .35	.60 (28) .32	.39 (3) .54	.41 (3) .53
MNT	1.0 (10) .0	.94 (24) .21	.80 (28) .36	-	-
HPT	.58 (1) -	.62 (1) -	.58 (1) -	0 (1) -	0 (1) -
RCP	-	.96 (7) .06	.62 (18) .45	-	-
RCM	0 (1) -	0 (1) -	.01 (1) -	-	-
MUT	-	-	-	-	-
PUT	.33 (36) .26	.35 (39) .29	.32 (38) .27	.15 (10) .12	.15 (11) .10
REP	-	-	-	-	-
STR	.27 (06) .25	.38 (6) .22	.45 (6) .32	.27 (1) -	.27 (1) -
CNV	.59 (8) .32	.47 (10) .37	.35 (11) .33	.24 (8) .15	.14 (8) .13
MWT	.47 (36) .43	.38 (41) .35	.30 (38) .30	.18 (39) .15	.20 (39) .15
CWK	.16 (76) .28	.21 (14) .35	.16 (83) .27	.21 (88) .14	.20 (90) .14
WAG	.43 (15) .44	.21 (14) .37	.32 (16) .42	.17 (16) .19	.11 (14) .16
POPULAR	.38 (289) .39	.39 (325) .37	.34 (391) .35	.23 (312) .21	.24 (308) .22
PROPERTY QUALI- FICATION	.31 (75) .38	.28 (93) .36	.40 (93) .36	.20 (80) .18	.23 (87) .20
APPOINTED	.35 (111) .40	.41 (133) .43	.38 (142) .41	.21 (92) .16	.20 (94) .17

Table 3-19

SALES REVENUE PROPORTION OF TOTAL
REVENUES BY TYPE OF DISTRICT

	S60 x̄ (N) s.d.	S64 x̄ (N) s.d.	S67 x̄ (N) s.d.	S68 x̄ (N) s.d.	S70 x̄ (N) s.d.
IRR	.51(100).35	.55 (96).33	.54 (96).32	.39 (94).30	.38 (94).29
CSA	-	-	.11 (04).12	-	.50 (04).35
MTR	-	-	-	-	-
CAL	.62 (50).43	.63 (73).42	.56 (84).41	.34 (67).39	.39 (66).39
MIM	-	-	-	-	-
CMS	.36 (63).41	.36 (85).40	.39 (97).39	.30 (08).23	.51 (52).29
CWT	.58(129).39	.59(139).36	.63(138).33	.41(160).32	.43(162).31
FCN	.03 (28).06	.04 (27).07	.09 (28).20	-	.51 (07).44
MNT	. -	.05 (26).20	.16 (27).33	. -	.01 (24).01
HPT	-	-	-	-	-
RCP	-	.02 (07).03	.08 (18).24	-	-
RCM	-	-	-	-	-
MUT	-	-	-	-	-
PUT	.62 (34).25	.54 (37).28	.53 (36).30	.58 (10).28	.51 (39).33
REP	-	-	-	-	-
STR	.73 (06).25	.59 (06).22	.50 (06).29	-	.69 (06).25
CNV	.34 (09).31	.34 (10).34	.52 (11).35	.30 (08).37	.52 (10).39
MWT	.31 (42).39	.43 (41).39	.54 (37).37	.39 (37).36	.35 (76).33
CWK	.77 (76).33	.73 (85).38	.76 (82).30	.39 (86).28	.41 (89).28
WAG	.50 (15).44	.58 (15).45	.49 (16).46	.45 (16).34	.41 (15).37
POPULAR	.48(338).40	.49(372).38	.51(392).37	.40(302).32	.42(360).31
PROPERTY QUALIFICATION	.59 (66).41	.49 (90).41	.55(102).40	.34 (76).38	.43 (83).39
APPOINTED	.52(115).44	.46(139).45	.50(138).42	.40 (90).30	.33(121).31

Table 3-20

DISTRICTS WITH SIGNIFICANT DIFFERENCES
BY COUNT (P ≤ .05)

	Sales Proportion	Levy Proportion	Administration Proportion
IRR		L60	
CSA			
MTR			
CAL		L64	
MIM			
CMS	S67	L64	A60, A64, A67
CWT	S60, S64, S67, S68, S70	L60, L64, L67, L68	A67, A68
FCN		L67	
MNT	S70		A64
HPT			
RCP		L64	
RCM			
MUT			
PUT		L64	
REP			
STR			
CNV			
MWT			A64
CWK		L60	
WAG	S60, S64, S68		
POPULAR	S60, S64, S67, S68	L60, L64, L67	A68
PROPERTY QUALIFICATION		L64	
APPOINTED			

Tables 3-11 and 3-12 above can be analyzed in combination with Tables 3-18 and 3-19 to determine the relative revenue sources for each type and category of district. Again we see that popular districts vary significantly according to population density, whereas this is not the case in either property qualification or appointed districts. Table 3-20 shows the specific districts that account for this significant variation.

Principal functions of the following districts are generally comparable according to the various provisions of the enabling acts: (1) Irrigation, California Water, and Water Storage Districts; and (2) Community Service, County Water, Public Utility; Municipal Water and County Waterworks. Comparison of similar types of districts by using the proportional figures presented above is somewhat limited. Further correlational analysis of California Water Districts and Irrigation Districts shows wide and significant differences in the correlation of levy revenues and total revenues. Additionally, there are significant differences in the stability of levy assessment revenue over time. The actual figures are presented below:

The correlation of levy revenue with total revenues:

Year	1960	1964	1967
Irrigation	.37	.35	.17
California	.57	−.08	.01

Levy revenue correlation over time:

Year	1960–64	1960–67	1964–67
Irrigation	.95	.91	.95
California	.58	.61	.91

The figures above indicate that levy revenue in Irrigation Districts is positively related to total revenue and is extremely stable over time. Levy revenue in California Water Districts, on the other hand, is less stable over time and since 1964 seems to be unrelated or, in other words, fluctuates randomly regardless of variations in total revenue. We may therefore conclude that the popularly elected Irrigation Districts tend to perform more consistently than property qualification California Water Districts.

Tables 3-21 and 3-22 indicate that the proportion of administrative expenditure is fairly consistent in all categories and types and in urban, suburban, and rural counties. In general, we observe that districts which are largely agricultural (as indicated in Table 3-21) tend to have lower administrative costs than districts which supply domestic services.

It is somewhat surprising to note that property qualification districts in urban counties exhibit the lowest scores, which probably

Table 3-21

ADMINISTRATIVE EXPENDITURE PROPORTION OF TOTAL
EXPENDITURES BY METHOD OF SELECTION OF
GOVERNING BODY AND BY TYPE OF COUNTY

YEAR	POPULAR			PROPERTY QUALIFICATION			APPOINTED		
	$\bar{x}$	(N)	s.d.	$\bar{x}$	(N)	s.d.	$\bar{x}$	(N)	s.d.
State Totals									
1960–61	.20	(318)	.22	.18	(69)	.20	.20	(118)	.22
1964–65	.20	(358)	.19	.14	(84)	.17	.21	(129)	.23
1967–68	.21	(370)	.19	.17	(96)	.22	.17	(138)	.30
1968–69	.24	(288)	.15*	.22	(91)	.21	.21	(87)	.12
1970–71	.24	(353)	.14	.21	(104)	.20	.19	(116)	.17
Urban Counties									
1960–61	.24	(237)	.20	.17	(38)	.22	.20	(104)	.22
1964–65	.23	(251)	.18	.12	(39)	.15	.20	(110)	.22
1967–68	.29	(242)	.22	.19	(40)	.22	.27	(102)	.27
1968–69	.23	(196)	.14	.20	(54)	.21	.22	(77)	.12
1970–71	.23	(221)	.12	.20	(55)	.21	.18	(101)	.17
Suburban Counties									
1960–61	.24	(78)	.23	.21	(28)	.18	.17	(14)	.20
1964–65	.24	(97)	.19	.18	(40)	.20	.22	(19)	.26
1967–68	.32	(92)	.25	.25	(37)	.28	.20	(17)	.29
1968–69	.23	(76)	.13	.23	(32)	.19	.17	(9)	.16
1970–71	.25	(109)	.13	.22	(43)	.19	.24	(12)	.21
Rural Counties									
1960–61	.19	(18)	.21	.17	(1)	–	.29	(2)	.41
1964–65	.18	(23)	.18	.33	(2)	.47	.40	(1)	–
1967–68	.19	(21)	.21	.50	(2)	.71	.46	(1)	–
1968–69	.32	(18)	.13	.13	(3)	.18	.14	(1)	–
1970–71	.25	(21)	.15	.09	(3)	.17	.38	(1)	–

* = $p < .05$

Table 3-22

ADMINISTRATIVE EXPENDITURE PROPORTION OF
TOTAL EXPENDITURES BY
TYPE OF DISTRICT

	A60			A64			A67			A68			A70		
	x̄	(N)	s.d.	x̄	(N)	s.d.	x̄	(N)	s.d.	x̄	(N)	s.d.	x̄	(N)	s.d.
IRR	.19	(76)	.24	.11	(80)	.14	.14	(81)	.17	.24	(91)	.18	.21	(93)	.17
CSA	.13	(2)	.06	.22	(2)	.04	.17	(3)	.17	.46	(1)	–	.20	(3)	.22
MTR	.42	(1)	–	.32	(1)	–	.34	(1)	–	.44	(1)	–	.58	(1)	–
CAL	.16	(51)	.22	.11	(66)	.15	.16	(77)	.22	.21	(80)	.21	.20	(86)	.21
MIM	.18	(1)	–	.	–			–			–		.44	(1)	–
CMS	.19	(65)	.23	.21	(83)	.20	.24	(95)	.22	.27	(12)	.14	.25	(58)	.12
CWT	.24	(131)	.21	.25	(142)	.19	.26	(134)	.17	.25	(145)	.12	.24	(152)	.12
FCN	.21	(27)	.23	.19	(25)	.22	.19	(27)	.19	.15	(2)	.07	.16	(7)	.19
MNT	.01	(10)	.01	.04	(22)	.12	.01	(26)	.03		–		.12	(24)	.21
HPT		–			–			–		.33	(1)	–	.34	(1)	–
RCP	.11	(2)	.09	.26	(8)	.28	.17	(16)	.24		–		.35	(8)	.17
RCM	.15	(1)	–	.14	(1)	–	.16	(1)	–		–		.26	(1)	–
MUT	.28	(1)	–	.16	(1)	–	.08	(2)	–		–		.13	(1)	–
PUT	.26	(38)	.17	.26	(41)	.17	.28	(41)	.22	.22	(11)	.14	.24	(42)	.14
REP		–			–			–			–			–	
STR	.30	(7)	.11	.42	(7)	.14	.38	(7)	.14	.50	(1)	–	.22	(7)	.07
CNV	.19	(10)	.15	.15	(10)	.20	.14	(11)	.16	.30	(9)	.18	.25	(10)	.21
MWT	.14	(41)	.20	.13	(42)	.14	.12	(39)	.12	.20	(39)	.17	.22	(38)	.18
CWK	.22	(81)	.22	.26	(82)	.23	.21	(84)	.21	.21	(84)	.12	.21	(84)	.15
WAG	.15	(13)	.18	.09	(14)	.14	.09	(13)	.17	.24	(13)	.16	.29	(13)	.16
POPULAR	.21	(318)	.22	.20	(358)	.19	.21	(370)	.19	.24	(288)	.15	.24	(353)	.14
PROPERTY QUALIFI-CATION	.18	(69)	.20	.14	(84)	.17	.17	(96)	.22	.22	(91)	.20	.21	(104)	.20
APPOINTED	.20	(118)	.22	.21	(129)	.23	.17	(138)	.20	.21	(87)	.12	.19	(116)	.17

indicates the use of contracted domestic retailers. This is the case in El Toro Water District, which has four customers: three agricultural and the Rossmoor Sanitation Company, a domestic retailer which supplies the water and sewage treatment services for nearly 50,000 residents. These residents therefore have no vote or influence in the operation of the district, except indirectly through the privately owned sanitation company.

We may therefore conclude that a low administrative expenditure proportion may indicate not only that a district is more efficient but also that it may be engaged in wholesaling activities.

Table 3-20 summarizes the analysis of variance findings of significant differences according to type of district. Popular districts vary on all three of the proportional measures, due largely to the performance of County Water Districts and to a lesser extent Community Service Districts. If we consider the relatively high amount of public participation in these two types of districts and the relative absence of public participation in property qualification and appointed districts, we may speculate on the possible meaning of this finding. Variations in population produce variations in the sales revenue of a water district. Levy rates will therefore be adjusted unless there exists heavy indebtedness and/or a lack of consideration for the residents, since levy assessments tend to be charged uniformly regardless of water consumption. In general, then, the revenue base of a district, if it is responsive to the residents, should vary according to variations in population density. This is the case in popularly elected districts but is apparently not a factor in property qualification and appointed districts.

Table 3-12 above indicates the nature of water sales revenue by type of county and by method of selection of governing body. It appears that domestic sales in property qualification districts are increasing, unlike both appointed and popularly elected districts. Water Conservation Districts (CNV), for example, have increased domestic sales from 13 to 21 percent.

Certain districts have made or are planning to make provisions which would change the method of selection of the governing board when population increases and changes in consumption patterns change the environment of the district. Property qualification districts with more than 50,000 inhabitants, for example, would vote on a one person/one vote basis rather than according to assessed valuation of property owned. Recent court decisions are

Patterns of Financial Performance: Correlation Analysis 87

supportive of this kind of reform. Our findings repeatedly show that variations in population density do not affect the behavior of property qualification districts and that participation by the public is either non-existent or extremely low in these types of districts. Also, domestic sales do tend to increase in such districts.

Table 3-15 above indicates a significant difference between popularly elected districts on the one hand and property qualification and appointed districts on the other. Popularly elected districts tend to allocate a larger proportion of their expenditures towards depreciation, amortization, and utility depletion additions. We may speculate that the relatively newer property qualification and appointed districts experience different budgetary criteria than popularly elected districts.

THE ANALYSIS OF EXTREME CASES

Tables 3-9 through 3-12 above can be used in a number of ways. To this point we have attempted to compare districts through the presentation of average numbers and proportions which indicate the typical score certain types of districts in certain locales possess. It is also possible to identify extreme cases for each of the computed variables and to compare the relative frequency of extreme cases in each type of district.

For example, districts with net profits that exceed 30 percent may be disproportionately occurring in a particular type of district and/or a particular locale. Los Alisos Water District in Orange County averaged around 50 percent profit in the fiscal years 1970–73 as indicated below:

Year	1970–71	1971–72	1972–73	1973–74
Total revenues	901,654	1,650,098	1,373,743	1,904,714
Total expenses	464,895	660,025	709,916	926,887
Net profit	436,759	990,073	668,827	927,827
Profit proportion of total revenue	48.44%	60.01%	48.51%	48.71%

Los Alisos is a property qualification district which anticipates participation in the Alisos Water Management Agency, a regional agency formed by the execution of a joint powers agreement of a number of districts and municipalities, the majority of which are governed by property qualification. The ability of this district to generate net income makes bond proposals unnecessary. Analysis of the net profit proportions in other Orange County districts, both popular and property qualification, indicates that the management of Los Alisos is significantly different.

Table 3-23 identifies the frequency of extreme levy revenue proportions. This table indicates that approximately one fourth of all water districts do not generate revenue by levy assessments. It must be noted that in this table, the figures for the individual types of districts are tentative at this point in time and are therefore suitable only for comparative purposes. However, this table is exemplary of our ability to tabulate the relative and actual frequencies of extreme scores by category for all of the Controller's variables as well as for our computed variables. Secondly, it is possible to individually identify water districts whose fiscal transactions seem extraordinary.

SELECTED REGRESSIONS

In this final part of this chapter, we will present some graphical views of certain relationships for one type of one person/one vote district (Irrigation) and for one type of property qualification district (California Water). In these particular cases, a small number of observations—for instance, Imperial Irrigation District—had such large values that it was not possible to plot the raw scores and make any sensible interpretation of them. Thus, in the tables that follow, we have taken the logarithm to the base 10 of each raw score. This allows us to reduce the impact of outliers on the scatter-plots to be examined and to make more sense of the data.

Let us turn to Figure 1, which presents the relationships between acreage and total revenues for Irrigation Districts. Note first of all that the plot exhibits a fairly general positive linear trend and that the correlation coefficient, while somewhat small, is statistically significant. Note also that the slope of the regression line indicates that for every unit change in the log of acreage, the log of total revenues will increase .29 times that unit increase. Finally, note that there are some districts, approximately 22 in number, that differ greatly in total acreage but have the same level of revenues. If we

Table 3-23

THE RELATIVE AND ABSOLUTE FREQUENCY OF DIFFERING LEVY REVENUE
PROPORTION LEVELS IN 1970 BY TYPE OF DISTRICT AND
BY METHOD OF SELECTION OF GOVERNING BODY

LEVY RATE PROPORTION	0	0 to .1	1. to .90	.9 to 1.0
IRR	20.2 (20)	12.1 (12)	67.7 (67)	0
CSA	--	--	--	--
MTR	0	0	100.0 (1)	
CAL	27.3 (21)	1.3 (1)	70.1 (54)	1.3 (1)
MIM	--	--	--	--
CMS	27.3 (3)	9.1 (1)	63.6 (7)	--
CWT	20.8 (33)	6.3 (10)	72.3 (115)	.6 (1)
FCN	--	--	--	--
MNT	--	--	--	--
HPT	100.0 (1)	0	0	0
RCP	--	--	--	--
RCM	--	--	--	--
MUT	0	0	100.0 (2)	0
PUT	18.1 (2)	9.1 (1)	72.7 (8)	0
REP	--	--	--	--
STR	--	--	--	--
CNV	12.5 (1)	37.5 (3)	50.0 (4)	--
MWT	23.9 (1)	0	76.9 (30)	0
CWK	15.6 (14)	15.6 (14)	68.9 (62)	0
WAG	50.0 (7)	14.3 (1)	35.7 (5)	0
ONE VOTE	12.2 (66)	7.4 (23)	71.1 (221)	.3 (1)
PROP Q.	25.6 (22)	4.7 (4)	68.6 (59)	1.2 (1)
APPOINTED	16.0 (17)	14.9 (14)	67.0 (63)	1.1 (1)

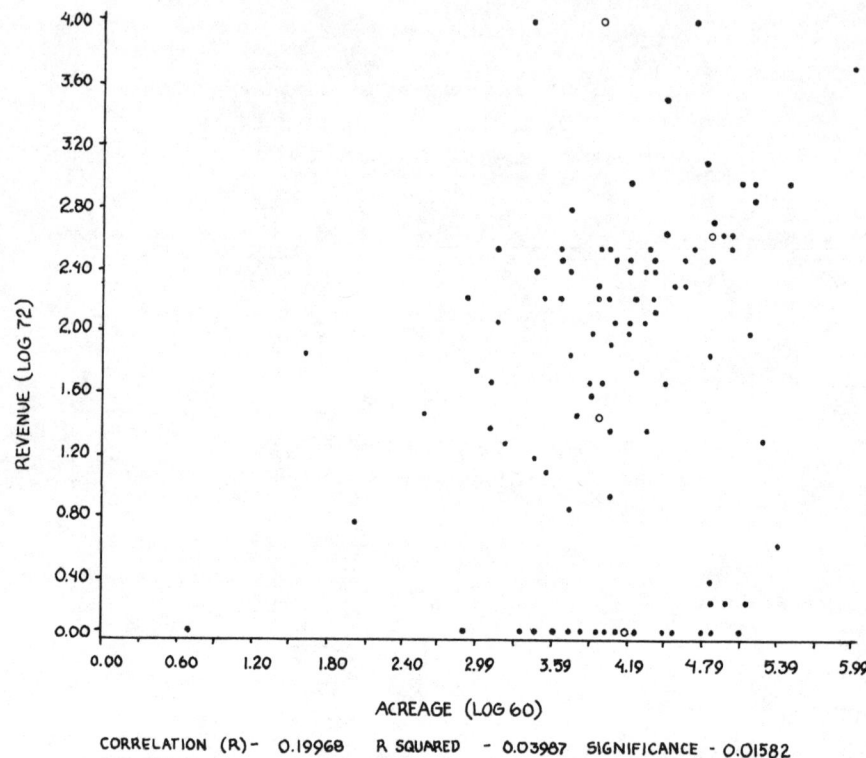

FIGURE 1. Revenue Plotted Against Acreage—Irrigation Districts

were to exclude these districts at the lower and upper ends of the revenue scale the linear fit would improve considerably. In general, then, Irrigation Districts experience about a 29 percent increase in revenue per acre of land service added.

Consider now Figure 2, which presents the same relationship for California Water Districts. In this instance, the correlation coefficient is lower than in the previous table, indicating, as does the scatter plot, that the relationship is weaker. In addition, the slope of the regression line is smaller, indicating that in California Water

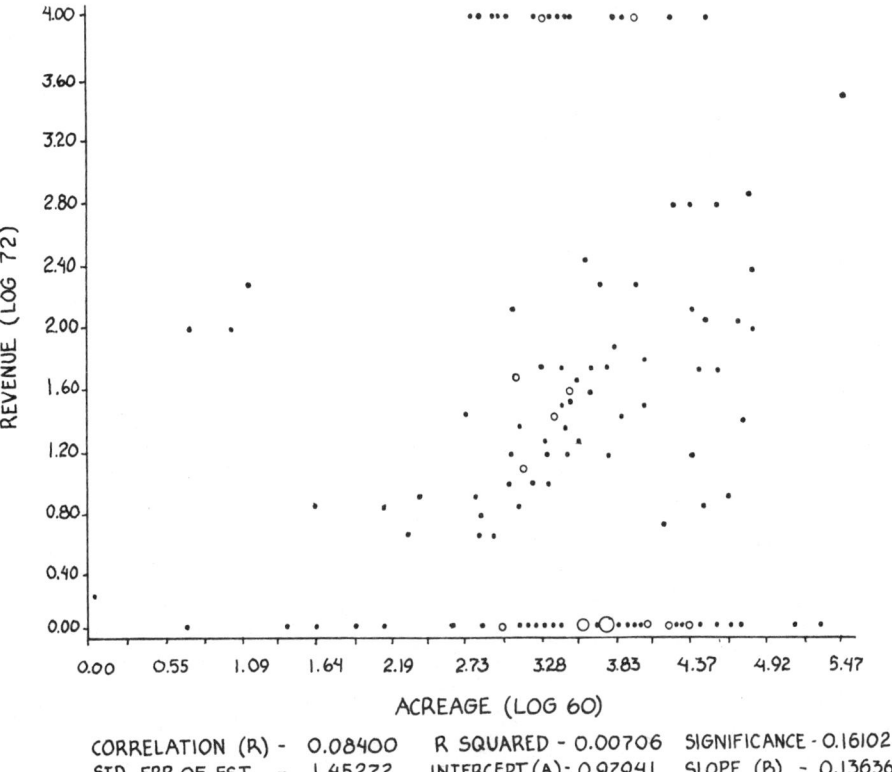

FIGURE 2. Revenue Plotted Against Acreage—California Water Districts

Districts the impact of acreage is less than in Irrigation Districts. The reason is fairly obvious from the plot. A very large number of California Water Districts are at the same revenue level, while their total acreage varies greatly. Approximately 73 California Water Districts are at the lowest or the highest point of the revenue scale, while these same districts are very much spread out on the acreage scale. Obviously, deleting these districts would improve considerably the linear fit in the plot.

Turn now to Figure 3, which plots total expenditures against

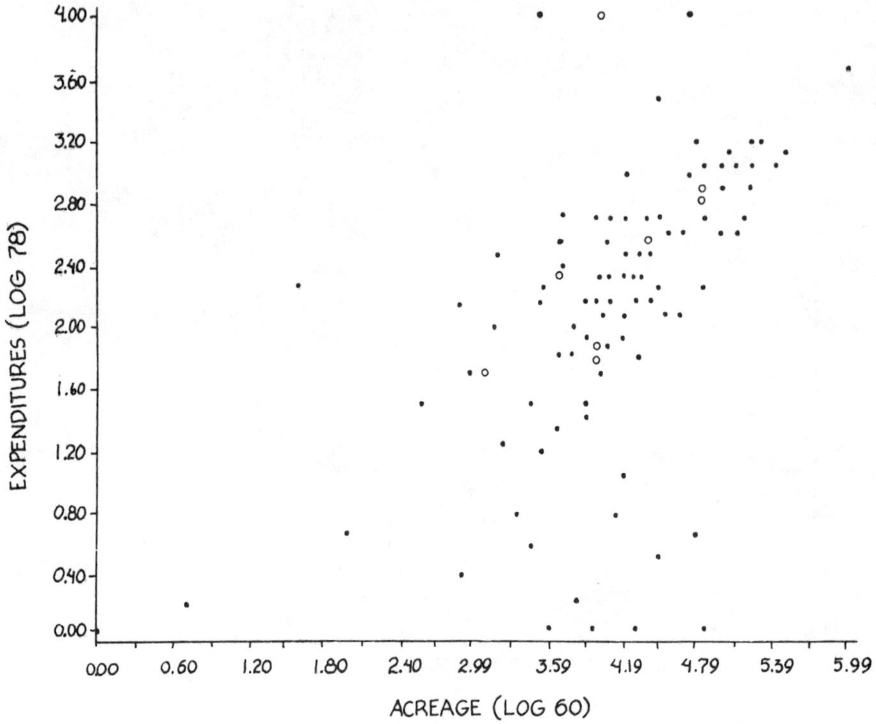

CORRELATION (R) - 0.43417 R SQUARED - 0.18850 SIGNIFICANCE - 0.00001
STD ERR OF EST - 0.93231 INTERCEPT (A) - 0.18909 SLOPE (B) - 0.53177

FIGURE 3. Expenditures Plotted Against Acreage—Irrigation Districts

acreage for Irrigation Districts. Similar results are obtained as in the previous two figures, with some notable exceptions. The relationship is again linear in a positive direction but both the slope and the correlation coefficient are somewhat larger than in Figure 2. The reason, which the plot indicates, is that there are many fewer Irrigation Districts which are at the same level of expenditures but differ greatly in acreage. Here the number is approximately 17.

Looking at Figure 4, which presents the same relationship for California Water Districts, the pattern for expenditures is more similar to that for revenues for these types of districts than for

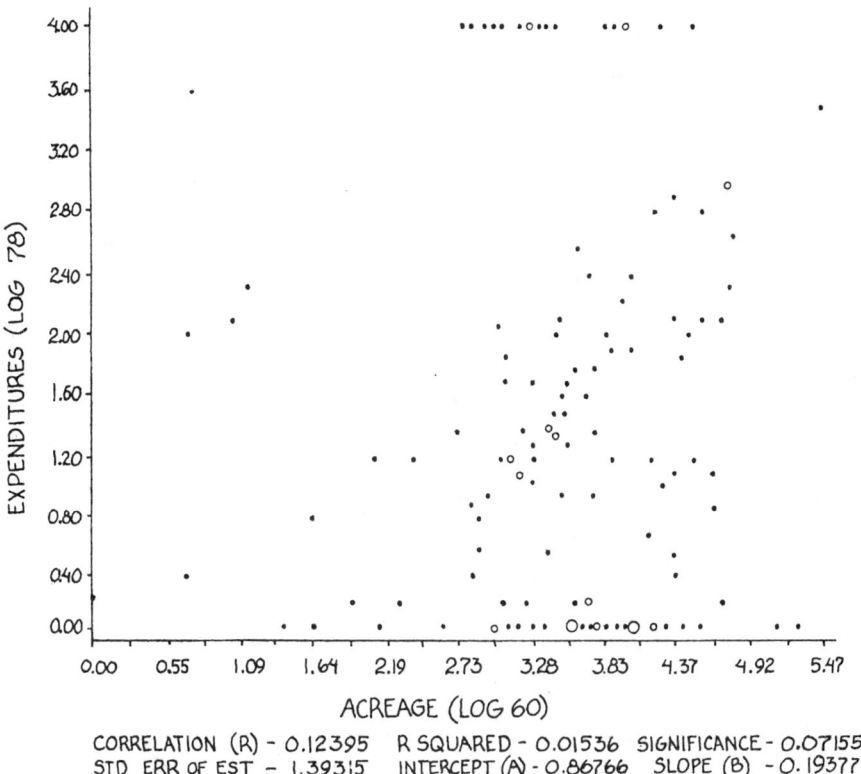

FIGURE 4. Expenditures Plotted Against Acreage—California Water Districts

Irrigation Districts. The degree of fit is weak and the slope quite shallow. In this instance better than 54 of the districts are at the same expenditure level (high or low), while their acreage varies considerably.

In general, then, for both types of districts, we note a positive linear trend for these variables examined. In three instances, there is a tendency for many districts to vary greatly in acreage but not in revenues. It is clear in these three instances that the degree of linear fit would improve greatly if these anomalies were removed from the analysis.

SUMMARY

We have classified districts by enabling act and by voting system and we have found dissimilarities in their patterns of financial performance. Most strikingly, those districts which provide for property-weighted voting exhibit relatively erratic financial behavior, with considerable oscillation over the 10-year period of our study. On the other hand, districts whose governing bodies are popularly elected or are appointed by county boards of supervisors display comparatively stable patterns of performance, their financial transactions over the decade tending to fall within fairly narrow ranges. Property qualification districts behave with wide variance in their financial transactions in both densely populated areas and lightly populated areas. Popularly elected and county board appointed districts tend to vary consistently according to variations in population density.

NOTES

1. In Tables 3-9, 10, 11, 14, 16, 18, and 19, each column is headed by an abbreviation which contains the first letter of the variable in the table and the year. Thus, in Table 3-9, the first column is headed by P60. This indicates that this variable is the Proportion of Total Revenue for 1960. This is the pattern for this and the other tables listed above.

2. In Table 3-10 and subsequent tables where we compare means and report a significance level at the bottom of the table, that significance level refers to the F Ration produced in Analysis of Variance and indicates the probability of being wrong in rejecting the null hypothesis that the three column means are not significantly different from each other. As a rule of thumb, any p value less than .05 indicates that the column means are significantly different from each other.

CHAPTER
4

A New Political Economy

Water districts are not isolated, self-contained public agencies. They interact with private economic institutions and their functions are often indistinguishable from those of locally influential private enterprise. Their activities need not be assessed from the perspective of economics alone. Districts take on distinctive political characteristics and district governing bodies determine who is going to pay the costs of development. In order to better understand the operations of water districts in California, we have supplemented the conventional tools of economics with essentially legal and political concepts and data. Our analysis is based on comprehensive 10-year financial histories of each of the approximately 1,000 special districts in the state which perform water utility functions. That information encompasses data on such matters as sources of revenue, patterns and levels of expenditure, growth trends in acreage, and assessed valuation. We have combined that economic information with such legal and political indicators as form of district governing body, type of enabling act selected by incorporators of the districts, the level of citizen participation in district elections, and patterns of incumbency. We have also considered the character of land ownership in each of California's water districts. Significant relationships between political and legal types of district and economic performance have been isolated. Ours is an essay in political economy. We believe our measures have enabled us to compare property qualification districts with one person/one vote districts and appointed districts at the state, regional, county, and local levels of aggregation.

Our statistical analysis yields consistent differences between property qualification districts and popularly elected, one person/one vote districts, along a number of political and economic dimensions. Specifically, we note that:

1. Although districts have grown both in number and size of budget between 1960 and 1976, property qualification districts have increased in number and size at a higher rate than either one person/one vote districts or county board-appointed districts.

2. The rate of growth in California Water Districts in terms of number of districts and budgetary components is significantly higher than any type of one person/one vote or appointed district. The budgetary growth of another type of property qualification district, the Water Storage District, is similarly phenomenal.

3. The property-weighted electoral system California Water Districts have grown primarily in water deficit areas of the southern and western San Joaquin Valley where land ownership patterns are characteristically corporate and large-scale. California Water Districts in such areas tend to be dependent for water delivery on federally-funded systems of dams and canals. Popularly elected districts are distributed fairly evenly throughout the state. County board-appointed districts tend to be located in the urban counties of California.

4. One person/one vote districts exhibit competitive electoral performance in combination with relatively stable fiscal performance to a far greater degree than do districts with property-weighted electoral systems. Property qualification districts continually exhibit a wider amount of variation in the majority of performance measures than do popularly elected and, to a lesser extent, county board-appointed districts.

5. The financial patterns of popularly elected districts vary according to their primary function and the population density of the area served. The financial performance of property qualification districts does not vary greatly even when those districts serve very

different kinds of users. Property qualification districts behave similarly in rural, urban, and suburban areas.

6. Property qualification districts tend to generate revenue by incurring debt, a tendency which is not characteristic of popular election districts. Indebtedness of property qualification districts is increasing more rapidly than in one person/one vote districts. California Water Districts account for a disproportionately large share of the total indebtedness of all water districts in the state.

7. The district which is able to defer payment on loans for capital development receives a higher rate of return on expenditures than a district which cannot make arrangements for future as opposed to current repayment of such loans. In California Water Districts, repayment on federal contracts has been deferred to the future. In such districts the burden of increased assessments will therefore fall on prospective owners.

We have measured change in reliance on state enabling acts, in systems of election, and in the financial and political performance of water districts. The provisions of the Irrigation District enabling act of 1887 were supportive of the family-size farm, the resident farmer, and the one person/one vote electoral system. By 1950 newer enabling acts had become prominent and these related closely to the activities of large-scale corporate agriculture and the interests of expanding suburban land use. Incorporation of districts under the property qualification acts was predominant in the 1950s and the 1960s. The Irrigation and Public Utility District acts are now of declining attractiveness as the corporate farm operator succeeds the farm settler. Our evidence for this conclusion is drawn from such measures as the incorporation of districts by type of enabling act, acreage and ownership patterns by type of district, irrigation sales by type of district, and the growth of non-agricultural functions by district type.

When we classified districts by type of voting system we found, as noted above, striking dissimilarities in their patterns of financial performance. Those districts which provide for property-weighted voting exhibit relatively erratic financial behavior with considerable oscillation over the 10-year period of our study. The volatile, irregular activity of the property qualification districts and the disparities which separate their operations from the relatively more consistent movement of other types of water districts are likely to persist. We have shown that where the franchise is open to all resident registered voters, elections are conducted more frequently and voter turnout is substantially higher than in districts with property-weighted electoral systems. Elections in the one person/one vote districts are more competitive and incumbency patterns are shorter. Such an electoral process is more likely to produce fairly representative, broad-based opinion on the district's governing body. In such districts, where divergent interests are present, there is a possibility that competing interests can be represented and eventually compromised and harmonized. That process, reflective of the extended range of interests in the community, can plausibly lead to relatively stable financial operations. Our evidence confirms that in such districts financial transactions tend to fall within fairly thin margins with relatively slight difference between the least and the greatest values. Where the governing body, as in property-weighted districts, is drawn from an unrepresentative group with parochial interests we observe irregular patterns of financial performance. In such a setting, the district board need not contend with contrasting policy views. Where a wide band of opinion drawn from all segments of the community is made available to a water district board, we find that the financial transactions of the board fall within moderate, relatively constant limits. Where a narrow band of opinion is found on the board, spasmodic ranges of financial conduct are likely.

In a property-weighted electoral system, where private and public interests are inseparable, owners of small holdings are likely to find it difficult or even impossible to appeal the decisions of a governing board. At times the control of public government—in this case the water district—by private organizations may be complete. There are serious economic and social consequences to a system which weights voting according to wealth. An illustration may be drawn from the recent history of a Water Storage District in the San Joaquin Valley. In a flood in 1969, one resident who was not a landowner found his house 15.5 feet below the water level of the crest of the flood—a flood that could have been contained. But the J. G. Boswell Corporation, the largest landowner in the district with 66,665 acres and holder of a simple majority of all votes, did not want the district to activate its flood-control machinery. To do so would have flooded Buena Vista Lake Basin, where the company has a long-term lease, and would have interfered with Boswell's agricultural operations. The company had the votes to forestall action. The Salyer Land Company initiated suit against the district as a result of the Tulare Lake Basin Water Storage District's decision to table a motion that would have provided for the diversion of flood waters to the Buena Vista Lake Basin. The case reached the United States Supreme Court.[1] Justice Rehnquist's majority opinion held that the activities of the district ". . .fall so disproportionately on landowners as a group that it is not unreasonable that the statutory framework focuses on the land benefited, rather than people as such."[2]

Rehnquist also noted that:

> Weighting the vote according to assessed valuation of the land does not evade the principle that wealth has no relation to voter qualifications where, as here, the expense as well as the benefit is proportional to the land's assessed valuation.[3]

In sum, Rehnquist held that the district did not possess enough power or provide general enough services to qualify as "governmental" and that since the special characteristics (i.e., property qualification) were reasonable, the court could only conclude that the equal protection clause was not violated. Justice Douglas' dissenting opinion contended that the duties and services offered by the district did indeed constitute vital and important governmental activity:

> . . .all the prospective victims of mismanaged flood control projects should be entitled to vote in water district elections, whether they be resident non-landowners, resident or non-resident lessees, and whether they own 10 acres or 10,000 acres. Moreover, their votes should be equal regardless of the value of their holdings, for when it comes to performance of governmental functions, all enter the polls on an equal basis.[4]

Douglas added that Water Storage Districts (and indeed all water districts in California) are considered exclusively governmental both legislatively and according to court interpretation. Douglas cited some of the powers that such districts possess, including eminent domain, tax-free construction debt privileges, and governmental immunity to suit.

In a more recent case, *Choudhry v. Free*,[5] a District Court in California ruled that the statutory requirement that candidates for board director be landowners was unconstitutional. That case involved the Imperial Irrigation District, the largest Irrigation District in the state. The court ruled that Imperial was exceptional in terms of services provided and population served. The Imperial

Irrigation District serves a large metropolitan area with electric power. Its governmental powers, however, are similar to those of other water districts in the state which employ property qualification voting systems.

Two contrasting political systems continue to share responsibility for California's water. One is based on popular elections and the other weights voting according to property owned. In California's rich agricultural lands two distinct economies have emerged. One tends to be characterized by family-size farming and the other is marked by large-scale and corporate farm ownership. There is evidence too that in the state's rural areas two dissimilar societies have taken shape. One is distinguished by farm communities and small businesses and the other is identified with extensive farming and non-resident ownership. The California Water District Act, along with other property-weighted enabling acts, has fostered a new political economy for California water.

NOTES

1. *Salyer Land Co.* et al v. *Tulare Lake Basin Water Storage District*, 410 U.S. 719 (1973).
2. *Ibid.*, p. 1228.
3. *Ibid.*, p. 1232.
4. *Ibid.*, p. 1235.
5. *Choudhry* v. *Free*, 552 P. 2d 438, 131 Cal. Rptr. 654 (1976).

APPENDIX A
Classification by Counties by Percent Urban*

Urban Counties	Percent Urban	Suburban Counties	Percent Urban	Rural Counties	Percent Urban
Alameda	99.0	Butte	63.8	Alpine	--
Contra Costa	93.6	Colusa	30.9	Amador	--
Fresno	75.1	Del Norte	38.9	Calaveras	--
Kern	80.2	El Dorado	41.8	Inyo	22.5
Los Angeles	98.7	Glenn	39.8	Mariposa	--
Marin	92.7	Humboldt	47.1	Mono	--
Monterey	74.6	Imperial	67.8	Nevada	19.8
Orange	98.8	Kings	54.9	Sierra	--
Riverside	78.6	Lake	29.9	Siskiyou	25.4
Sacramento	95.1	Lassen	39.3	Trinity	--
San Bernardino	89.8	Madera	49.1	Tuolumne	14.0
San Francisco	100.0	Mendocino	34.5		
San Joaquin	76.9	Merced	50.0		
San Luis Obispo	75.5	Napa	57.9		
San Mateo	98.3	Placer	40.5		
Santa Barbara	88.5	Plumas	29.6		
Santa Clara	97.5	San Benito	42.0		
Santa Cruz	75.0	Shasta	49.6		
Solano	92.8	Sonoma	58.6		
Stanislaus	69.9	Sutter	52.6		
Ventura	92.4	Tehama	38.3		
Yolo	75.4	Tulare	43.8		
Yuba	71.4				

Source: County and City Data Book, 1975

*The basic definition of urban population comprises all persons living in incorporated places of 2500 inhabitants or more.

APPENDIX B
Methodological Note

We present a variety of types of data and a number of different ways in which that data may be analyzed. We deem it important to discuss some methodological aspects of our work. We now summarize briefly the statistical procedures we employ.

Our project works with a basic data set of information contained in annual reports of the State Controller on over 1,000 special districts which perform water functions. The data set contains over 100 variables which deal with various financial and political aspects of district functioning. These include such matters as types of expenditures, types of revenues, capital outlays, etc. In addition, we have computed composite scores for such matters as administrative expenses. The basic set of variables is described in an appendix. The various composite scores will be described when they are discussed.

We have already described the bases on which we have classified water districts. In much of what follows, we will be presenting comparisons of districts in terms of arithmetic means on relevant variables. Other statistical techniques have been employed for describing various relationships and these are discussed below.

Averages and Dispersion

In order to differentiate among districts, we calculated a large number of arithmetic means for the different variables. For instance, in comparing one person/one vote (OPOV) districts with property qualifications (PQ) and County Board Appointed (APP) on the question of total debt, we found that for 1970 OPOV had an average debt of 1207.952, while PQ had 1185.87 and APP had 1164.209. Thus, on the surface, one would conclude that differences among the three types of voting systems did not produce large differences in total debt.

The figures were obtained by means of the following formula:

$$\bar{x} = x_1 + x_2 + \cdots + x_n = \sum \frac{x_i}{n}$$

where the x_i refer to individual districts and n refers to the total number of districts involved. This score can be thought of as representing the most typical score for a particular variable; say, total debt. A question that naturally arises deals with how big a difference is significant?* If we were dealing with random samples drawn from populations of interest, this question could be answered statistically by computing what is called a t-test for the difference between two means. Such a test requires that one calculate the difference between the two means and divide that difference by a measure of *expected* variability appropriate for such a difference. One factor which plays an important role in this calculation is called the standard error of the mean and is given by the following:

$$S_{\bar{x}} = \frac{S_{x_i}}{\sqrt{n}}$$

It will be noted that the number of observations, n, plays an important role here. As n increases, $S_{\bar{x}}$ decreases, all other things being equal. The end result is that rather small absolute differences can prove to be statistically significant. A rule of thumb here is that a difference between two means need be only twice its associated variance to achieve statistical significance. Consider the following hypothetical example in which a large n, say greater than 30, produces a small variance for the difference between two means, say, a variance as small as 1.5. Such a small variance would result in an absolute difference between two means of 3.0 proving to be statistically significant. The main point here is that, in most of our tables, we will be dealing with a rather large number of districts. Thus, a good portion of the differences will prove to be statistically significant even when the absolute differences are small. To avoid confusing the discussion, we will not focus on statistical significance but rather will attempt to identify substantive differences which are important.

In order to compare districts we will from time to time employ a measure of dispersion or a measure of how different the districts are from each other. This measure, termed the variance, basically takes each score for each district and, by subtracting each of these scores from the mean of all the districts on a variable and squaring that difference, produces an "average squared deviation around the mean." Arithmetically, the measure of dispersion looks as follows:

$$s^2 = \sum \frac{(x_i - \bar{x})^2}{n}$$

where x_i refers to each district score, $\bar{x}$ is the mean for all districts and n is the total number of districts involved. Frequently, one wishes to work with a measure of dispersion in the original unit rather than the square of those units. To do this one produces the standard deviation by taking the *square root* of the variance which produces the standard deviation. Thus, where the mean provided a score which indicated how alike the districts were on a variable, the standard deviation provides a score which tells us typically how each district differs from all of the rest. The larger the standard deviation for a particular variable, the more dissimilar are the districts on that variable.

We noted earlier that we will be examining the differences among means for different types of districts in order to determine if there are some relationships between the type of district and patterns of performance on different variables. We will also use three other techniques to identify relationships (or the absence of relationships) among our variables. These techniques are regression and correlation analysis and analysis of variance.

In regression analysis, we explore the extent to which one variable can be thought to cause another variable in terms of the amount of effect that the first has on the second. In this type of analysis, we obtain two things of interest: first, a slope of the regression or least squares line which tells us the *amount* of effect that the first variable has on the second. Second, we are able to plot the relationships in a scatter-plot which allows us to visually determine the nature of that relationship.

Appendix B: Methodological Note

The general form that regression takes is the following:

$$y_i = a + bx_i + e_i$$

where y_i is the actual score on the dependent variable, a is the point at which the least squares line intercepts the y axis, x_i is the score on the dependent variable, b is the slope of the least squares line or the amount of effect of x on y and e_i is an error term which summarizes those factors other than x which may have an effect on y. It is assumed that the factors in e_i are random and relatively unimportant. As we will note below, this type of analysis allows us to explore the causal connection between y and x in terms of the amount of change to be expected in y *per unit change in x*.

In the process of fitting a regression line to a set of data one question that naturally arises concerns the degree to which the least squares line "fits the data well." Put another way, unless the data are completely randomly distributed, it is possible to fit a least squares or regression line to them. The slope of that line, b, will be useful, however, only in those cases in which the data are grouped rather closely around the regression line. As part of regression analysis, it is possible to generate a measure of the extent to which the regression line is, in fact, a good measure of the relationship between x and y. This measure, called the correlation coefficient, is a measure of the spread of the individual x-y pairs around the regression or least squares line.

Arithmetically the correlation coefficient is given by the following formula:

$$r_{yx} = \frac{\sum (x_i - \bar{x})(y_i - \bar{y})}{\sqrt{\sum (x_i - \bar{x})^2} \sqrt{\sum (y_i - \bar{y})^2}}$$

In words, this measures the extent to which y and x co-vary, normed by the total amount of variation in both x and y. The correlation coefficient, r_{xy}, has a lower bound of -1 and an upper bound of 1 and as it approaches either of these bounds, we can say that the spread of the x-y points around the least squares line or the regression line is very close. Alternatively, as r_{xy} approaches zero, we can say the relationship between y and x is not a very good one.

If we think in terms of the fact that there is a total amount of variation in y (given by $\sum (y_i - \bar{y})^2$, we can interpret the correlation coefficient as a measure of the amount of variation in y that can be attributed to x. If the correlation between y and x is −1 or 1, x completely determines y. If it is less than ±1, the amount of variation in y that can be attributed to x is given by r^2_{xy}.

The final mode of analysis we will use is called analysis of variance. In the procedure, it is assumed that we have a dependent variable which is interval in character; that is, that it is a true metric. The independent variable, on the other hand, is nothing more than a set of nominal classes. In our research, as noted above, we have divided districts into three types of voting systems: one person/one vote, property qualification, and county board appointed. These three classes will be our independent variable, while patterns of financial performance will be our dependent variable.

In essence, this mode of analysis is an extension of the comparison of two means to detect significant differences. Here, we will be comparing more than two means in order to determine if there are important differences between the means for each class. Substantively, if we find such differences, we will be able to argue that that type of voting system has an effect of financial performance. We illustrate this type of analysis with specific examples.

APPENDIX C
List of Variables

This appendix lists the variables which we have used in this analysis of water districts in California. All of the data have been taken from the California State Controller's reports for the period 1960–71. The first entry is the variable number as used in our study (e.g., VAR019). The second entry is generally the year (e.g., 1960–61). The third entry is the variable name (e.g., REVENUES, TOTAL).

VAR001, COUNTY CODE NUMBER
VAR002, TYPE OF GOVERNING BODY
VAR003, TYPE OF DISTRICT
VAR004, 60-1 DEBT, TOT OUTST LONG-TERM
VAR005, 64-5 DEBT, TOT OUTST LONG-TERM
VAR006, 67-8 DEBT, TOT OUTST LONG-TERM
VAR007, 60-1 GEN REVENUE BONDS OUT
VAR008, 64-5 GEN REVENUE BONDS OUT
VAR009, 67-8 GEN REVENUE BONDS OUT
VAR010, 60-1, DEBT, OTHER OUT LONGTERM
VAR011, 64-5 DEBT, OTHER OUT LONGTERM
VAR012, 67-8 DEBT, OTHER OUT LONGTERM
VAR013, 60-1 UNMATURED GEN OBLIG BONDS
VAR014, 64-5 UNMATURED GEN OBLIG BONDS
VAR015, 67-8 UNMATURED GEN OBLIG BONDS
VAR016, 60-1 ACREAGE
VAR017, 64-5 ACREAGE
VAR018, 67-8 ACREAGE
VAR019, 60-1 REVENUES, TOTAL
VAR020, 64-5 REVENUES, TOTAL
VAR021, 67-8 REVENUES, TOTAL
VAR022, 60-1 REVENUES, ASSESS LEVIES
VAR023, 64-5 REVENUES, ASSESS LEVIES
VAR024, 67-8 REVENUES, ASSESS LEVIES
VAR025, 60-1 REVENUES, SERV CHARGES
VAR026, 64-5 REVENUES, SERV CHARGES
VAR027, 67-8 REVENUES, SERV CHARGES
VAR028, 60-1 REVENUE, OTHER
VAR029, 64-5 REVENUE, OTHER

108 Appendix C: List of Variables:

VAR030, 67-8 REVENUE, OTHER
VAR031, 60-1 SECURED RATE OF LEVY
VAR032, 64-5 SECURED RATE OF LEVY
VAR033, 67-8 SECURED RATE OF LEVY
VAR034, 60-1 EXPENDITURES, TOTAL
VAR035, 64-5 EXPENDITURES, TOTAL
VAR036, 67-8 EXPENDITURES, TOTAL
VAR037, 60-1 EXP, OPER, MAIN AND GEN
VAR038, 64-5 EXP, OPER, MAIN AND GEN
VAR039, 67-8 EXP, OPER, MAIN AND GEN
VAR040, 60-1 EXP, PAY ON FED CONTS
VAR041, 64-5 EXP, PAY ON FED CONTS
VAR042, 67-8 EXP, PAY ON FED CONTS
VAR043, 60-1 EXP, CAPITAL OUTLAY
VAR044, 64-5 EXP, CAPITAL OUTLAY
VAR045, 67-8 EXP, CAPITAL OUTLAY
VAR046, 60-1 EXP, GROSS PAYROLL
VAR047, 64-5 EXP, GROSS PAYROLL
VAR048, 67-8 EXP, GROSS PAYROLL
VAR049, 68-9 INDEBT, TOT OUT LONGTERM
VAR050, 70-1 INDEBT, TOT OUT LONGTERM
VAR051, 68-9 DEBT, OTHER LONGTERM
VAR052, 70-1 DEBT, OTHER LONGTERM
VAR053, 68-9 DEBT, UNMAT GEN OB BONDS
VAR054, 70-1 DEBT, UNMAT GEN OB BONDS
VAR055, 68-9 REVENUES, FROM LEV ASSESS
VAR056, 70-1 REVENUES, FROM LEV ASSESS
VAR057, 68-9 LEVY, RATE PER 100
VAR058, 70-1 LEVY, RATE PER 100
VAR059, 68-9 ACREAGE
VAR060, 70-1 ACREAGE
VAR061, 68-9 SALES, RESIDENTIAL
VAR062, 70-1 SALES, RESIDENTIAL
VAR063, 68-9 SALES, BUSINESS
VAR064, 70-1 SALES, BUSINESS
VAR065, 68-9 SALES, INDUSTRIAL
VAR066, 70-1 SALES, INDUSTRIAL
VAR067, 68-9 SALES, IRRIGATION
VAR068, 70-1 SALES, IRRIGATION
VAR069, 68-9 SALES, FOR RESALE
VAR070, 70-1 SALES, FOR RESALE
VAR071, 68-9 REVENUES, TOTAL OPERATING
VAR072, 70-1 REVENUES, TOTAL OPERATING
VAR073, 68-9 EXP, GEN AND ADMINIS
VAR074, 70-1 EXP, GEN AND ADMINIS

Appendix C: List of Variables: 109

VAR075, 68-9 EXP, DEPREC AND AMORT
VAR076, 70-1 EXP, DEPREC AND AMORT
VAR077, 68-9 EXPENDITURES, TOT OPERATING
VAR078, 70-1 EXPENDITURES, TOT OPERATING
VAR079, 68-9 REVENUES, NON-OPERATING
VAR080, 70-1 REVENUES, NON-OPERATING
VAR081, 68-9 EXPENSES, NON-OPERATING
VAR082, 70-1 EXPENSES, NON-OPERATING
VAR083, 68-9 EXPENSES, UT PL DEP ADD
VAR084, 70-1 EXPENSES, UT PL DEP ADD
ID5, PAGE NUMBER FIVE OF DATA
VAR101, 67-71 DIRECTORS, NUMB APPOINT
VAR102, 67-71 DIRECTORS, NUMBER ELECTED
VAR103, 67-71 DIRECTORSHIPS, NUMB AVAIL
VAR104, 67-71 DIRECTORSHIPS, NUMBER OF CAN
VAR105, 67-71 VOTING, AGGREGATE PERCNT

APPENDIX D
Variables and Formulae Used in Chapter 3

In Chapter 3 we presented a series of analyses which were computed from our original variables. We present in this appendix a list of how these variables were computed. In order to assist the reader in identifying these computed variables, we will give two illustrations. Consider first the variable "Depreciation and Amortization." This variable is computed by summing VAR075 and VAR077 (Expenditures, Depreciation and Amortization–1968–69 and Expenditures, Total Operating–1968–69) and dividing this total by VAR075, thus producing a computed measure of depreciation and amortization. As a second example, consider the variable "sales revenue proportion." For 1960–61, this involves dividing revenues, service charges by total revenues. In this manner the reader can go through these computed variables to determine how they were constructed.

COMPUTED VARIABLE*	YEAR	DERIVATION
1. Net Income - Loss	1960-61	019 - 034
	1964-65	020 - 035
	1967-68	021 - 036
	1968-69	(071 + 079) - (077 + 081)
	1970-71	(072 + 080) - (078 + 082)

* In these computation a slash (/) indicates "divided by"

Appendix D 111

COMPUTED VARIABLE	YEAR	DERIVATION
2. Sales Revenue Proportion	1960-61	025 / 019
	1964-65	026 / 020
	1967-68	027 / 021
	1968-69	(061 + 063 + 066 + 068 + 069)/(056 + 072 + 080)
3. Levy Revenue Proportion	1960-61	022 / 019
	1964-65	023 / 020
	1967-68	024 / 021
	1968-69	055 / (055 + 077 + 079) (056 + 078 + 080)
4. Administrative Revenue Proportion	1960-61	046 / 034
	1964-65	047 / 035
	1967-68	048 / 036
	1968-69	073 / (073 + 077)
	1970-71	074 / (074 + 078)
5. Depreciation & Amortization	1968-69	075 / (075 + 077)
	1970-71	076 / (076 + 078)
6. Utility Plant Depletion-Addition Expense Propoertion	1968-69	083 / (083 + 077)
	1970-71	084 / (084 $\pm$ 078)
7. Domestic Sales Proportion	1968-69	(061 + 063 + 065) /(55 + 71 + 79 + 61 + 63 + 65)
	1970-71	(62 + 64 + 66) / (56 + 72 + 80 + 62 + 64 + 66)
8. Irrigation Sales Proportion	1968-69	067 / (067 + 069 + 071 + 080)
9. Revenue	1960-61	019
	1964-65	020
	1967-68	021
	1968-69	071
	1970-71	072

Appendix D

COMPUTED VARIABLES	YEAR	DERIVATION
10. Expenditures	1960–61	034
	1964–65	035
	1967–68	036
	1968–69	077
	1970–71	078
11. Indebtedness	1960–61	004
	1964–65	005
	1967–68	006
	1970–71	050
	1960–61	016
	1964–65	017
	1967–68	018
	1968–69	059
	1970–71	060

APPENDIX E
Abbreviations of Districts Used in Tables

IRR — Irrigation
CSA — County Service Areas
MTR — Metropolitan Water
CAL — California Water
MIM — Municipal Improvement
CMC — Community Services
CWT — County Water
FCN — Flood Control and Water Conservation
MNT — Maintenance
HPT — Harbors and Ports
RCP — Recreation and Parks
RCM — Reclamation
MUT — Municipal Utility
PUT — Public Utility
REP — Water Replenishment
STR — Water Storage
CNV — Water Conservation
MWT — Municipal Water
CWK — County Water Works
WAG — Water Agency or Authority

Index

Abbreviations of districts used in tables, 113

Acreage of districts, 32, 34-35; correlation analysis by political systems, 56-57; correlation analysis by type of county, 62, 64; correlation of expenditures, 63-64; correlation of indebtedness, 59, 61; correlation with revenues, 62; by type of district, 32, 34-35; by type of enabling act, 32; by type of political system, 47, 50-51

Administration of water resources, 5

Administrative expenditures, 83-85

Age of districts in correlations of budgetary components, 57

Agencies responsible for water resources, 5

Agrarian versus urban use, 3-4

Agricultural settlements, 5; corporate holdings, 3, 4, 97, 100; effect of scale of operation on community organization, 5; family-size, 3, 100; irrigation agriculture, 3-4, 13

Alisos Water Management Agency, 87

Analysis of variance statistical technique, 59, 106

Appointed districts *see* County board appointed districts

Berrenda Mesa Farming Company, 25

Berrenda Mesa Water District, 21, 25-27, 58, 73

Blackwell Land Company, Inc., 25

Blackwell Management Company, 25

Bond issues, 58; California Water Districts, 20

Boswell, J. G., Corporation, 21, 98-99

Buena Vista Lake Basin, 99

California Water acts, 9; *see also* Enabling acts

California Water Districts, 63; acreage and revenues, 90-93; corporation farms, 21; enabling act requirements, 11; federally funded hydraulic systems, 4; financial performance, 33, 46, 47; financial reporting to State Controller, 30; formation, 20; governing boards, 20; indebtedness, 97; levy revenues, 83; powers and services, 20; property ownership requirements, 10-11, 18, 30; property qualification voting, 4, 16, 20; rate of growth, 96; special improvement districts, 20; water utility function, 16

California Water Districts Act, 20; number of districts, 10

Capital outlay, 46-47

Choudhry v. Free, 99

Citizen participation, 5, 16-25; appointed directors districts, 18; popularly elected districts, 18; property qualification districts, 18

Classification of districts, 27-28; by enabling acts, 4-16; by voting system, 16-25, 97

Community organizations, effect of scale of agricultural operations on, 5

Community Services Acts, 9

Community Service Districts, 7, 9-10; financial performance, 33; number of districts, 10; profit-loss comparisons, 77; property ownership requirements, 10

Competition for scarce water resources, 3

Corporate farm operators, 3, 4, 21, 97, 100

Correlation analysis; administrative expenditures, 83-85; analysis of extreme cases, 87-88; computed indicators, 67; expenditure measures, 73-87; indebtedness, revenue, expenditures, and acreage, 54-66; revenue measures, 67-73; selected regressions, 88-93

Counties, classification of, 101

County and City Data Book, 25, 59

County board appointed districts, 16; citizen participation, 18; financial performance, 31, 47, 53

115

County Service Areas; appointed directors, 16; enabling acts, 9; financial performance, 47
County Water Districts; enabling acts, 9-10; popularly elected officials, 16; profit-loss comparisons, 77
County Water Districts Act, 9-10; number of districts, 9-10
County Waterworks Districts, 9

Debt: correlation analysis, 54-66; correlation analysis by type of county, 65-66; correlation analysis by type of political system, 61; property qualification districts, 97; by type of district, 42-43, 46; by type of political system, 48, 51
Drought (1975-1977), 3

El Toro Water District, 86
Elections, water districts, 5, 16-25
Emergency regulations, 3
Enabling acts for water district organization, 4-16; California Water, 9; California Water District Act, 20; Community Services, 9; County Service Area, 9; County Waterworworks Districts, 9; effect of, 97; elections of directors, 18; financial performance and, 32-47, 53; formation of districts, 7-10; incorporation by decade and type of act, 7-8; landowner participation, 10; Municipal Water, 9; property ownership as requirement for voting, 10-12; types of, 6-8; voting requirements, 10-12; Water Storage District Act, 21; Wright Act of 1887, 4, 7
Expenditures, 73-87; administrative, 73, 83-85; capital outlays, 46-47, 49; correlation analysis, 73-87; depreciation and amortization, 73, 76; profit-loss comparisons, 77-78; total, 46; by type of county, 64-66; by type of district, 44-46; by type of political system, 48, 51, 58, 60; utility plant depletion, 73, 76-77

Farms and farming: corporate ownership, 3, 4, 97, 100; family-size, 3, 100
Federal agencies, 5
Federal service areas, 28
Federally-funded systems, 4, 96
Financial performance: acreage, 32, 47; Controller's data, 29-31, 53-54; correlation analysis, 53-94; correlation analysis of revenue, expenditure, debt and acreage, 54-66; debt, total, 46, 48; description and trends, 29-52; district revenues, 32-33; enabling acts and, 32-47, 53; expenditures, 48-49; fiscal allocation patterns, 53; profit-loss comparisons, 77-78; rate of levy, 33, 40-41; revenue from assessment levies, 33, 48; total expenditures, 46, 48; total revenue (operating), 47-48; by type of county, 77, 79; by type of political system 55-57
Financial reporting, 29-31; change of format, 30-31
Financial transactions, 98
Fire protection services, 16-17
Flood Control and Water Conservation Districts, 7
Flood control problems, 98-99
Formation of districts, 7-10, 13

Geographic settings of water districts, 5, 12-13; incorporation of districts, 13-15; regional distribution, 25-27
Governing bodies, 5, 16-25, 95, 98; California Water Districts, 20; enabling acts, 9; property-weighted systems, 98
Governmental responsibilities, 13

Harbor and Ports Districts, appointed directors, 16
Hydraulic systems, federally funded, 4, 97

Imperial Irrigation District, 88, 99-100
Institutional setting of water development, 3-28
Irrigation Districts, 13; acreage, 32, 88, 90; domestic and industrial water, 9; elections, 18; expenditures plotted against acreage, 91-92; family-size farms, 4; financial performance, 32, 33, 46, 47; financial reporting, 20, 30; levy revenues, 83; number of districts, 9-10; popularly elected directors, 4, 16; profit-loss comparisons, 77; property ownership requirements, 10; Wright Act of 1887, 4, 7
Irvine Company, 21
Irvine Ranch Water District, 21, 63

Land and water use, 5
Landowner participation, 9-10
Levies: assessment of, 68, 73; rates of, 33, 40-41, 86; revenues from, 33, 38-39, 74-75, 79-80, 83; by type of political system, 48, 50
Library services, 16-17
Los Alisos Water District, 87-88

Maintenance Districts, appointed directors, 16
Metropolitan Water Districts, 7; acreage, 32; appointed directors, 16; financial performance, 32, 47
Municipal agencies, 5
Municipal Improvement Districts, 7
Municipal water departments, 7
Municipal Water Districts; enabling act, 9; financial performance, 46-47

One person/one vote districts, 16, 27, 47; citizen participation, 18; compared to property qualification districts, 96-97; correlation analysis, 54-66; elections, 18-19; financial patterns, 96-97; financial performance, 31, 47, 53, 57, 96; Irrigation Districts, 4; stable fiscal performance, 96

Police protection, 16-17
Political decision systems, 47
Popularly elected districts *see* One person/one vote districts
Privately-owned agencies, 5, 7
Property qualification districts, 10-13, 16, 27, 29; citizen participation, 18; compared to one person/one vote districts, 96-97; correlation analysis, 54-66; effect of standby levy, 73; elections, 18-20; financial performance, 31, 47, 53-54; indebtedness, 97
Public Utility Districts, 7, 9-10, 32; elections, 18; number of districts, 9-10; one person/one vote, 16; financial performance, 32, 47

Reclamation Districts: enabling acts, 10-11; property ownership requirements, 10-11
Recreation and park programs, 16-17
Recreation and Parks Districts, 7
Regional distribution of water districts, 25-27
Revenues: correlation analysis, 60, 62, 65, 67-73; district, 32-33; from levies, 33, 38-39, 48, 53, 68, 73-75, 79, 80, 83, 89; net income-loss revenue, 68-69, 78; operating and non-operating, 32-33, 47-48; sales or service charges, 53, 68, 70-72, 81, 86; sources of, 67-68; by type of county, 62, 65; by type of district, 32-33, 36-37; by type of political system, 47-48, 50, 60
Rossmoor Sanitation Company, 86

Sacramento Valley, 3
Salyer Land Co. v. Tulare Lake Basin Water Storage District, 98-99
San Joaquin Valley, 3-4; California Water Districts, 96
San Luis Project, 4
Sewage treatment services, 86
Social policy decisions, 58
Special act districts, 7; water utility functions, 5-6
State agencies, 5
State Controller: change of format, 30; financial reporting to, 30-31; Report data, 29-31
State service areas, 28
Statistical procedures, 102-12; analysis of variance, 59, 106; averages and dispersion, 102-6; correlation coefficient, 104-6; list of variables, 107-9; regression analysis, 104-5; variables and formulas, 110-12
Suburban counties, 25; revenue and expenditures, 59-60
Supreme Court decisions, 99

Tulare Lake Basin Water Storage District, 21, 99

Urban counties, 25, 101; revenue and expenditures, 59-60
Urban development and water distribution, 3, 13

Voting patterns, 97-98
Voting requirements, 10-11, 13
Voting systems, 16-25, 97; appointed directors, 16; one person/one vote, 16; property qualifications, 4, 16, 20

Waste disposal, 16-17
Water Agency districts, 7, 46-47
Water Conservation Districts, 10-12, 86
Water districts: abbreviations used in tables, 113; average size, 32; enabling acts, 4-16; incorporation, 8, 12-13; new political economy, 95-101; number of, 5-6; regional distribution, 25-27; services, 5, 10-11, 16-17; types of, 6-7
Water Storage Districts, 21-24, 99; elections, 22-24; enabling acts, 10-11, 21-24; financial performance, 33; property ownership requirements, 10-11, 16, 21
Westlands Water Districts, 4, 20-21
Wright Act of 1887, 4, 7

About the Authors

Merrill R. Goodall is Professor of Government at the Claremont Graduate School in California. He has held senior United Nations appointments, directed an international assessment of community development in South Asia, and in 1952 was the first western advisor to the Government of Nepal. He has published extensively on water institutions in California.

John D. Sullivan is Associate Professor of Political Studies at Pitzer College and Chairman of the Master of Arts Program in Public Policy Studies at Claremont Graduate School. He is the author of numerous articles and co-author of *Unity and Disintegration in International Alliances*. His research interests include the application of social science methodologies and computer simulation to the analysis of public policy problems.

Timothy De Young is Assistant Professor of Political Science at Behrend College of the Pennsylvania State University. As a Peace Corps volunteer in Nepal he devised irrigation systems at the village level. His Ph.D. thesis at the Claremont Graduate School dealt with water districts in California. Among De Young's current interests is coastal zone management.

Professors Goodall, Sullivan, and De Young have contributed testimony on irrigation institutions at Senate Interior Committee hearings. They have taught courses on resource management and have conducted institutes on California water development.